Totally dairY-Free Cooking

LOUIS LANZA

AND LAURA MORTON

WILLIAM MORROW AND COMPANY, INC. NEW YORK

This book is dedicated to my parents, Frank and Patricia Lanza. When I opened Josie's Restaurant in 1994, my parents said that a health food restaurant would never work on the Upper West Side of Manhattan. Nevertheless, they supported me emotionally and financially. And for that I will be eternally grateful.

Library of Congress Cataloging-in-Publication Data

Lanza, Louis.
      Totally dairy-free cooking / Louis Lanza and Laura
Morton.
          p.   cm.
      ISBN 0-688-16909-0
      1. Milk-free diet Recipes.   I. Morton, Laura, 1964– .
II. Title.
RM234.5.L36   1999
641.5'63—dc21   99–30472
                    CIP

Printed in the United States of America

First Edition

2 3 4 5 6 7 8 9 10

BOOK DESIGN BY DEBBIE GLASSERMAN

www.williammorrow.com

Contents

Acknowledgments

I'd like to thank everyone at William Morrow for believing in this project from the very beginning. To my editor, Justin Schwartz: Your hard work and keen insight helped this book be its best. Thanks to my agent, Dan Strone, for all of your wonderful support.

I'd also like to thank my family for all of their love and support over the years. To my brother Jim, who introduced me to health food. To my brother Anthony, the ultimate taste tester and a true dairy lover (if he likes my dairy-free recipes, everyone will). To my Uncle Frank, a great baker, a gifted artist, and the giver of the best advice. To my Grandpa Lanza, whose moderation and temperance influence my thinking every day of my life. Some of my fondest memories of childhood are the days I watched Grandma Josephine, the namesake of my restaurants Josephina and Josie's, cook our big family dinners. She was my greatest inspiration to become a chef.

I want to thank my dogs, Mario and Juice, for their unconditional love, their comic relief, and for never complaining when I had them try the leftovers!

To my good friends Dr. Marc and Karin Wilk and Dr. Andrew Kornstein. Thanks for all your motivation, inspiration and support. Also, I want to thank my good friend Jules Klapper and his

Cutting Edge catalog, whose vast knowledge of health, nutrition and holistic therapy has kept me up to the minute on the latest breakthroughs. And thanks to my friends Norah and Vinny Downey: Your invaluable advice and honest palates helped me so much during the recipe development process. Thank you to Dr. Philip Anthony and Alice Trigiani for keeping my body in tune throughout this project with your wonderful homeopathic healing and for never saying no whenever I needed food tasters! Danny Deutsch, friend and project tester on the results of eating well and exercise: Thanks for trusting me. Many thanks to my friend Philip Kessler, party promoter extraordinaire, for keeping my social life active during the everyday long hours of working the restaurants and during the writing of this book.

A lot of people helped build my dream over the years, and without their help, I could never have finished this book. I am especially fortunate to have an outstanding partner, Cheng Meng Ling, who always tells me how things are behind the scenes—whether good, bad or ugly. I also want to thank Ricky Yeo, my partner and *chef de cuisine* at Josie's. You've helped me maintain a consistent product day in and day out. Thanks for helping me standardize many of the recipes for this book. Your contribution was a huge addition. Thanks to my good friend and business partner, Rob Morrow. Your belief in Josie's and our philosophy about food has helped me build a dream come true. Thanks to William and Carol Vinci, my restaurant design team and good friends. You always bring a warm feeling into our dining rooms with your brilliant designs and use of color. And to everyone at the Health Nuts, for always keeping my pantry full and being there when I needed that emergency ingredient.

To my assistant, Barnny: Thanks for all of the extra time and effort you put in on this project. To Jim Sperber, thanks for your attention to detail and all of the research you did on validating the important details of this book. To my coauthor, Laura Morton, thank you for your determination and dedication to help me make this dream come true.

I couldn't have done this without all of you. Please accept my gratitude and appreciation.

Foreword

Lactose intolerance is defined as the inability of our gastrointestinal tract to absorb the carbohydrate lactose. Lactose happens to be the major "building block" of milk and hence all milk-based products. Lactose intolerance occurs when our digestive tract fails to produce the enzyme lactose. This malfunction, though genetic in nature, can begin as early as the first day of life and affects anywhere from 30 to 50 million Americans. Symptoms can range from minimal to life threatening and include abdominal pain, flatulence, cramping and diarrhea. Many cases of *mild* lactose intolerance are never recognized and may plague the victim for a lifetime. Diagnosis is simple and can be made by either a blood test or a hydrogen breath test.

The condition, while not lethal in the developed world, does however result in unnecessary morbidity for those undiagnosed sufferers.

Medical science has yet to find a cure, and present therapy is based on either lactose enzyme replacement or lactose-free diets. The former is only partially successful whereas the latter has, until now, been difficult to adhere to, given the near universal use of milk and milk-based products in our diet.

Louis Lanza's *Totally Dairy-Free Cooking* is a thorough, well–written and meticulously researched cookbook that makes a lactose-free diet palatable to both sufferers and nonsufferers alike. *Bon Appétit!*

Albert B. Knapp, M.D., F.A.C.P.
Associate Physician, Section of Gastroenterology,
Lenox Hill Hospital
Clinical Assistant Professor of Medicine, New York University
School of Medicine

Foreword

Introduction

For the most part, people aren't aware of the amount of dairy products they consume on a daily basis. By the time the average American reaches fifty, he or she has consumed enough milk and dairy to equal the cholesterol contained in one million slices of bacon. According to one study, most Americans eat around two and a half pounds of dairy and dairy-based products every day!

Humans were never meant to consume dairy products! We are the only species that drinks the milk of another animal. The exception to this, of course, is domesticated cats, which consume cow's milk only because we feed it to them, despite the fact that veterinarians strongly discourage this. In fact, cows don't even drink milk when they get older! They get their calcium from eating grass.

It's true that milk is rich in many nutrients, especially calcium and vitamin D. One of the questions I'm frequently asked is "what about calcium?" The recommended daily allowance of calcium for most adults is 800 milligrams. That's the amount contained in 2½ cups of whole milk, 4 ounces of hard cheese, or more than a quart of ice cream or cottage cheese. You can get the same amount of calcium by drinking 7 ounces of calcium-enriched orange juice or eating 2¼ cups of broccoli—or from a calcium supplement containing elemental calcium. Cows don't get calcium from milk, so why should you? Although tens of millions of dollars are spent every year touting the virtues of milk, the truth is that the calcium in cow's milk is much coarser than in human milk, and the human body does not adequately absorb it. Since pasteurizing, homogenizing, and other processing methods reduce the amount of calcium in dairy products, it becomes difficult to use these as a good source of calcium. Pasteurizing milk destroys the vitamins in it, especially vitamin D. That's why dairies have to artificially add back vitamin D, an essential vitamin that regulates the absorption of dietary calcium in our bodies. Without vitamin D, any effort we make to absorb calcium is useless.

There are a lot of foods that are better sources of calcium than milk. Many of the recipes in this book use calcium-rich tofu. Fish, especially salmon, is a great source of calcium. Spinach, broccoli and all other green leafy vegetables contain calcium, as do nuts and sesame seeds. Fruits such as dates, figs and prunes offer up enough calcium for your body's needs. The following chart shows the amount of calcium present in a variety of foods.

C A L C I U M I N F O O D S	
Vegetables*	**Calcium (mg)**
Broccoli (1 cup)	178
Brussels sprouts (8 sprouts)	56
Carrots (2 medium)	38
Cauliflower (1 cup)	34
Celery (1 cup)	54
Collards (1 cup)	336
Kale (1 cup)	206
Onions (1 cup)	58

* Unless otherwise specified, vegetables are raw.

Totally dairy-free Cooking

Potato, baked (1 medium)	20
Romaine lettuce (1 cup)	20
Squash, butternut (1 cup)	84
Sweet potato, baked (1 cup)	70
Spinach (1 cup)	68
Turnip greens	268

Legumes	
Chickpeas (1 cup)	78
Great Northern beans (1 cup)	121
Green beans (1 cup)	58
Kidney beans (1 cup)	50
Lentils (1 cup)	37
Lima beans (1 cup)	52
Navy beans (1 cup)	128
Peas, green (1 cup)	44
Pinto beans (1 cup)	82
Soybeans (1 cup)	175
Turtle beans, black (1 cup)	103
Tofu (½ cup)	258
Vegetarian baked beans (1 cup)	128
Wax beans (1 cup)	174
White beans (1 cup)	161

INTRODUCTION

* 3

Grains	
Brown rice (1 cup cooked)	23
Corn bread (2-ounce piece)	133
Corn tortilla (1 medium)	42
English muffin (1 medium)	92
Pancake mix (¼ cup, or 3 pancakes)	140
Pita bread (1 piece)	31
Wheat bread (1 slice)	30
Wheat flour, all-purpose (1 cup)	22
Wheat flour, calcium-enriched (1 cup)	238
Whole wheat flour (1 cup)	49
Calcium fortified cereal, e.g., Total (1 cup)	300

Fruit	
Apple (medium)	10
Banana (medium)	7
Figs, dried (10 medium)	269
Orange, navel (1 medium)	56
Orange juice, calcium fortified (1 cup)	300
Pear (medium)	19
Raisins (⅔ cup)	53

4 *

Protein Group	
Sardines, canned with bones (3 ounces)	372
Salmon, canned with bones (3 ounces)	165
Tofu, processed with calcium (4 ounces)	145

I know, you're probably thinking you could never go totally dairy-free. You're saying things like, "I could never give up milk in my coffee" or "No way will I give up cheese!" Or, "What about an occasional bagel with cream cheese?" This book isn't about total *elimination* initially, but rather, *moderation*. The recipes have been created to show you that cutting back on your dairy intake isn't as hard as it seems. Although this book gives you more than one hundred recipes that are totally dairy-free, I am not suggesting that you have to give up dairy completely. Knocking out 75 percent of the dairy products you eat will set you on the right path to living a healthier life. So if you want to have a crème brûlée for dessert one night, go ahead! An occasional slice of pizza? No problem! (Although you might find that you enjoy a soy cheese pizza just as much.) The overall idea is to start cutting back on your dairy intake until it becomes an easy way of life.

What's so important about dropping dairy from our diets? There are a lot of valid reasons to explore a dairy-free lifestyle, but for most people, cutting down on the amount of dairy consumed will have great health benefits. One of the most noticeable will be an overall leaner appearance and a reduction in your body fat. By cutting back and eventually eliminating dairy from your diet, you're automatically reducing your fat intake. Excluding dairy products clearly helps reduce cholesterol levels, thereby decreasing the risk of heart disease. The fat and cholesterol contained in milk is a real one-two punch to the human body.

Since our bodies don't have the necessary enzymes to break down and properly digest dairy products, it makes perfect sense that we would have an adverse reaction to eating foods that contain dairy, a condition known as being "lactose intolerant." Lactose intolerance is defined as lacking the ability to digest lactose, the predominant sugar found in all dairy products. It's estimated that more than fifty million Americans have this problem. In fact, the number is probably even higher, yet most are unaware of the condition. This inability to digest food puts an unnecessary strain on your digestive system.

Studies have shown that nondairy eaters have a better cardiovascular status than dairy eaters do. A diet that is high in dairy is also likely to be associated with an iron deficiency because cow's milk is very low in iron. Frighteningly, ovarian cancer has been linked to a diet high in dairy. According to a recent Harvard study, the body cannot properly break down the enzymes found in milk, and when dairy consumption exceeds the enzymes' capacity to break down galactose (the sugar that results when lactose is broken down in the body), there is a buildup of galactose in the blood. This is believed to have an adverse effect on a women's ovaries. The real problem is from the milk sugar, not the milk fat, so women who eat lowfat or nonfat products like cottage cheese and yogurt are actually at greater risk because the bacteria used in manufacturing these foods increases the production of galactose.

Since milk is one of the most common food allergies, respiratory problems, canker sores, diarrhea or constipation, skin conditions and other allergic reactions can occur as a result of eating foods that contain dairy. Unfortunately, most people don't even know they have a sensitivity to dairy. They think that their reactions are normal, and without ever giving their bodies a break, how would they ever know they are not? To date, no treatment exists to improve the body's ability to digest dairy foods except to change one's diet. What's the best way to do that? To cut back and eventually eliminate dairy from your diet.

Everyone can benefit from incorporating dairy-free recipes into their life whether or not they are truly lactose intolerant. There is no downside to eliminating dairy. Dairy-free living is not just a choice. For most people it's a necessity, whether they know it or not. I am offering you some easy-to-use alternatives so that you can get started on learning how to cook dairy-free.

This book represents fourteen years of my professional life. As the owner and chef of Josie's, New York's premier dairy-free restaurant, I have successfully combined the atmosphere of a fash-

Totally
daiRY-free
Cooking

ionable New York Grand Café with the appeal of healthy dairy-free cooking. You might say I have cross-pollinated the cheeseburger lover with the strict vegetarian to effectively create a new breed of consumer. One of the main ingredients in our continued success as a restaurant is that we focus on flavor and consistency. I have created and perfected hundreds of delightful, delectable and, yes, dairy-free alternatives to all of your favorite dairy filled recipes. The days of dull and tasteless health food are over! People won't eat food that will help them live a healthier happier life if it doesn't taste good. The recipes in this book focus on pleasing even the most discriminating palate, offering the same high-flavor meals found in my restaurant. Whether you are a mainstream gourmet or a health-conscious consumer, each and every recipe will, I hope, inspire you to live a healthier life.

It's interesting to watch people experience dairy-free cooking for the first time. If I don't tell people their meal is dairy-free, they often never know. If I put a bowl of soy ice cream and a bowl of frozen yogurt in front of you, I'm willing to bet that you'd go for the soy ice cream in a taste test. In fact, I prepared a soy ice cream sundae with Soy Caramel Sauce (page 225) for Rosie O'Donnell. Rosie ate the sundae in front of millions of her viewers, and she couldn't tell the difference.

Imagine if all of the great chefs in the world were told they could no longer use dairy in their cooking: no butter, no cheese, no milk or cream. What a struggle it would be to alter their fat-laden, over-buttered and cheesy recipes. I face that challenge as a chef every day. I replace the cream in my New England–Style Clam Chowder, take the "milk" out of chocolate and substitute the cheese in my grilled cheese, all without forfeiting flavor or satisfaction.

This book is about *replacing* the flavors added by dairy without *sacrificing* the taste of your food. Your palate will accept subtle changes in the way you eat, especially when you don't feel like you're giving up delicious flavors. You ought to be able to enjoy the food you eat. It's one of life's great pleasures. Have fun experimenting with these new flavors and ingredients. You might just find you've been missing out on something after all!

HOW TO STAY DAIRY-FREE WHILE DINING OUT

Most restaurants use dairy products to help make meals look more appealing and appetizing. Chefs will glaze a little butter over pasta just before serving it to give it a sheen. If you ever order roasted chicken in a restaurant, chances are that the chef rubbed a little butter between the skin and the meat to keep the chicken moist and tender. There are all sorts of little tricks that chefs use that affect what you eat. If you're going dairy-free and you want to stay that way while eating out, the most important thing to do is to spend a few minutes before you go out and write down exactly what you *don't* want in your food. Write a list that says "no butter, no milk, no cream, no cheese." Put it on an index card and make copies so you always have one with you when dining out. Make it as simple and easy to read as possible. Also include a list of acceptable substitutions and then give it to your food server, and say, "I would appreciate it if the chef could make some dairy-free suggestions using these guidelines." The chef's not intentionally going to serve you something that you don't want to eat. Food servers don't always know exactly what each menu item contains so they may give you misleading information just to get the order in. You could end up eating the things you don't want. As long as you're specific, the chef will make suggestions that in most cases will happily oblige your request. Any restaurant that declines to accommodate your simple guidelines may not be worthy of your business.

THE PERFECT KITCHEN

Like anything we do in life that requires making a change, the more prepared we are to implement that change, the easier the transition. Having all of the tools and foods easily within your reach will make the cooking process easier and more enjoyable.

Having the proper equipment in your kitchen is very important. For example, make the investment in a good quality nonstick pan that will last. If you buy an inexpensive one, the coating may wear through or start peeling after using it just a few times. A good electric handheld blender will be very useful in preparing many of the

Totally dairy-free Cooking

recipes in this book and you'll find it's a lot easier to clean than a conventional blender or food processor. The following list contains the items that are the bare essentials in any kitchen. Go through the list and see which items you already have and make a note of the items you might want to buy.

The Perfect Kitchen—Essential Equipment

Box grater

Can opener

Cheesecloth or fine-mesh strainer (chinois)

Coffee grinder

Colander

Electric handheld mixer (cordless or traditional)

Food mill

Food processor

Good-quality cutting board

Good-quality nonstick skillets/frying pans (10-inch and 12-inch)

Heavy glass mixing bowls

Juicer

Knife sharpener, steel and stone

Measuring cups

Measuring spoons

Nonstick baking sheet

Nonstick grill pan

Nonstick loaf pan

Nonstick wok

Pepper mill

Pizza stone

Plastic or stainless steel mixing bowls

Pyrex baking dish

Roasting pan

Salad spinner

Saucepans/stockpots (various sizes), stainless steel preferable

Sharp knives, including serrated

Spatula, plastic and long-handled metal

Steamer

Tongs

Vegetable peeler
Vegetable scrub brush
Water filter
Wooden spoons (various lengths)

THE PERFECT PANTRY

In addition to mentioning all the proper equipment for your kitchen, I've made a list of some essential items you will want to have in your pantry. You certainly don't have to fill your cupboards with all this at once, but as you start to eliminate an old product, such as refined white sugar, replace it with a better choice, like organic sucanat or start buying soy milk when you run out of regular milk. Next time you buy a box of pasta, try one of the recommended brands from this list. The important thing is to try these new foods and see which ones you like. You'll find that many of these brands are slightly more expensive because they don't use any artificial, less costly fillers often found in mainstream products. It's worth spending a little more on these items because ultimately the flavor is more intense and you won't need as much of the product to satisfy your taste. I recommend using organic products whenever possible.

Most people think a steak is a steak, a tomato is a tomato, and a chicken is a chicken. But considering the huge amounts of artificial hormones and chemicals used to raise and grow the cattle, produce and poultry, it's important to understand that this is far from reality. If you eat products that contain these drugs and chemicals, it's bound to have an effect on you. I started thinking about healthy alternatives so that I could still enjoy meat and poultry from time to time. I started researching products and found that almost everything we eat, from meat to vegetables, is chemically treated or enhanced one way or another. Organic and free-range products have to be farmed according to certain strict guidelines.

Organic Foods

"Organic" is a method of producing foods using no synthetic fertilizers and pesticides. Organic is not a type of food. There has been quite a bit of controversy surrounding the FDA regulations of a standard definition for nationwide classification of organic foods. To date, seventeen states have various guidelines that qualify a food as "organic." Organic foods used to be hard to locate outside of major urban areas, but at least 50 percent of the supermarkets in America now have an "organic foods" section. Buying a product that says "certified organic" is the best insurance that you are getting a truly organic product. This means that the farmers' crops were grown in soil that has been free of prohibited synthetic pesticides for at least three years. It also means that the farmer is actively nurturing additional land so it will be fertile and plentiful for future generations' food needs. Processed foods that meet the requirements can also be labeled as organic. In order to be classified as such, at least 95 percent of the ingredients have to be grown and processed according to the FDA standards to earn that label.

When meats are labeled "certified organic," it means the livestock was raised on only organic feed, without growth hormones or antibiotics, and were treated humanely while being raised.

Sometimes organic foods aren't as appealing to the eye and might not last as long as nonorganic products, but their flavors are abundant.

Until federal regulators implement national standards on organic foods and reassess the use of pesticides on crops, make sure to thoroughly wash all produce with a produce cleanser before eating it. Don't assume that organic food is truly organic unless it has been certified. The same holds true for "free-range" products such as meat and poultry. "Free-range" is defined as meat and poultry that are raised on natural grains without the use of any artificial hormones or antibiotics, and are allowed to run free as opposed to being inhumanely caged.

Food is like fuel to our bodies. If you buy cheap gas for your car, it doesn't perform as well. The higher the octane, the better the performance. Why would you skimp on the quality of fuel that you put into your body? A healthful diet begins with healthful foods, which are cleaner, meaning they are not as processed or refined. The purer the ingredients you use the cleaner the food. Once you discover the alternatives, it actually becomes as easy to buy the organic versions as the other brands.

Beans
These are the brands of cooked beans that I recommend for ease and speed when cooking. Make sure to rinse the beans, before using.

Eden Organic or Westbrae Natural—kidney beans, black beans, white beans, black soybeans, garbanzo beans, chickpeas, lentils, red beans

Cheese Substitutes—see page 18

Condiments
These are more healthful versions of many mainstream condiments. Next time you run out of your old standby, try replacing that product with one of these.

Muir Glen Organic tomato products and ketchup

Hain, Westbrae and Grey Poupon mustards

Hain Eggless Mayonnaise Dressing

Soyco Foods Lite and Less Soy Parmesan

Soymage Soy Parmesan

Vogue Organic Instant Base Bouillon

Kikkoman Lite Soy Sauce

Bragg's Liquid Amino—A very pure fermented soybean product used like soy sauce when diluted with water. It has a strong flavor so make sure you taste test it before using.

Dr. Bronner's Soy Sauce Replacement—Most soy sauces are made with wheat unless specified. Dr. Bronner's and Bragg's are both wheat-free.

The American Miso Co.—Miso is fermented soybeans. This company makes six or seven flavors including barley, chickpea and plain.

Maine Coast Kelp—Excellent to spice up any of your favorite soup broths.

Soymage Lowfat Sour Cream Alternative

Eden Arrowroot—Used as a thickener replacing cornstarch.

Sushi Chef Wasabi—A hot Japanese mustard powder.

Totally dairy-free cooking

Sushi Chef Mirin—A sweet rice wine.

China Bowl Chili Puree with Garlic

Westbrae Wheat-free Tamari—A premium soy sauce that comes from the top of the barrel in the fermentation process.

Eggs—see page 19

Grains

I firmly believe in using only organic products for environmental and health reasons and grains are no exception. These are quality brands with the best reputations in the industry and are certified organic.

Neshaminy Valley

Shiloh Farms

Lowell Farms

Arrowhead Mills

Jaclyn's Organic Bread Crumbs

Juices/Frozen Fruit

All of these companies offer organic juice with no processed sugar added. It's the closest thing to drinking freshly squeezed juice and it's very easy to find.

Sirreal

Santa Cruz Organic

Eden Organic

Hain

Solano Gold

After the Fall and R. W. Knudsen—Both of these companies make great carbonated fruit juice drinks, their version of soda.

Cascadian Farms, organic frozen fruit—This is an excellent product for baking and making fruit smoothies.

Meat Substitutes

When prepared properly, these meat substitutes will fulfill any craving you have for that meat flavor and texture without giving up any of the protein.

Nasoya Tofu

White Wave Tofu

Now Foods Textured Vegetable Protein (TVP)—TVP comes in many forms, from granules to chunks. It simulates meat. You can buy plain, beef- or chicken-flavored TVP. While plain TVP is low in sodium, be aware that some companies inject a lot of sodium when they add the beef or chicken flavor. You can marinate TVP and use it in a stir-fry in place of meat.

Fearn Soy Granules—This is similar to TVP.

Lightlife Tempeh, Fakin Bacon/Fakin Bacon Bits—Lightlife is a premium company with one of the biggest selections of meat substitute products. Tempeh is a fermented soy product which combines some other ingredient, usually quinoa or wild rice with soy and compresses it. It has a firm texture and a very good flavor.

Milk Substitutes—see page 18

Oils

All oils start off in fine condition. However, the transportation and storage can spoil the oil. Heat and light can turn an oil rancid. Oil should be stored in a glass container in a cool dark place, preferably not too near your stove. The most important thing to look for is that it is a naturally pressed oil.

Hain/Spectrum/Eden—extra-virgin olive oil, canola oil and safflower oil

Pastas

De Boles—This organic pasta company produces durum semolina and Jerusalem artichoke flour pastas as well as the new corn flour pasta and rice flour pasta, both of which are wheat-free.

Westbrae Natural

Ancient Harvest Quinoa—Give this a try if you want something new but note that the texture won't be the same as regular pasta.

Lundberg Family Farms Organic Brown Rice Pasta

Totally dairy-free cooking

Seasonings

I recommend Spice Garden brand for nonirradiated dried spices and seasonings.

- Sage
- Chili powder
- Ground ginger
- Cinnamon
- Vegetarian Worcestershire sauce—Regular Worcestershire sauce is made with anchovies. This is not, which makes it 100 percent vegetarian.
- Sea salt
- Fresh ground pepper (white, black)
- Red pepper flakes
- Hot sauce
- Paprika
- Minced garlic
- Dill weed
- Oregano
- Fresh basil leaves
- Cumin
- Curry powder
- Fresh parsley
- Ground coriander
- Cardamom
- Cloves
- Thyme
- Shallots
- Turmeric
- Poppy seeds
- Horseradish
- Frontier Natural Flavor Alcohol-Free vanilla/almond extracts
- Mushrooms
  - Cremini
  - Portobello
  - Shiitake

Spreads

These are the least refined versions of some of the most popular commercial spreads. The flavors are pure and have the largest amounts of the ingredient you're paying for. For example, commercial peanut butter has oil, sugar and salt whereas organic peanut butter is 100 percent peanuts.

Shedd's Soybean Margarine—This is the best replacement for butter.

Arrowhead Mills Organic Peanut Butter—This brand has no sugar, salt or oil added. It is 100 percent peanuts.

Tree of Life Organic Tahini—Tahini is a ground sesame seed spread. It can be used like peanut butter.

Cascadian Farms Organic Fruit Spread and Sorrell Ridge Fruit Spread—These two products have no processed or refined sugar added. Even some of the pure fruit spreads add refined sugar so these are really a better choice.

Stocks

When you don't have time to make your own.

Westbrae or Hain and Pacific Foods—All make excellent chicken, beef and assorted vegetable stocks.

Sugar Substitutes

Wholesome Foods Sucanat—an organic, naturally milled cane sugar juice with molasses

Florida Crystals Evaporated Cane Sugar—dried cane sugar juice without the molasses

Spring Tree Pure Maple Syrup

Shady Maple Farms Organic Maple Syrup

Honey Brother Honey

Eden Organic Barley Malt Syrup—The process of sprouting barley turns starch to sugar. Use 1:1 in recipes to replace honey and molasses. To replace sugar, use ¼ cup less liquid for each cup of barley malt.

Sunspire or Tropical Source Dairy-Free Chocolate Chips—These chocolate chips are made with chocolate (made with unrefined cane sugar juice), cocoa butter, tofu, lecithin (a soy derived emulsifier) and vanilla bean.

Lundberg Family Farms Organic Brown Rice Syrup—Made with organic brown rice, water and less than 1 percent natural fungal enzymes. Brown rice is ground to a meal, cooked to a slurry, mixed with a small amount of fungal enzymes. This process converts the starches to natural sugars.

Wax Orchards Concentrated Fruit Juice Blend—Liquid fruit sweetener concentrate syrup from pear, peach, pineapple and/or apple. This is an especially good sugar replacer for cold drinks and cold sauces because it blends so easily.

Fruit Source Liquid Fruit/Grain Sweetener

Teas

Eden

Traditional Medicinals

Garden of the Andes

Celestial Seasonings Organic

Vinegars

All of these vinegars use only organic ingredients.

Eden Organic—rice wine, cider, balsamic, white or red

Ohsawa *Ume*

Mitoko *Umeboshi* Paste

UNDERSTANDING THE DIFFERENT DAIRY ALTERNATIVES

There are many dairy substitutes available on the market today. Soy, rice, oats and almonds are all used to make dairy substitute products. Giving up dairy only means that you're giving up products that come from a cow or another animal. There are lots of good alternatives readily available from various food sources. Companies such as the Hain Food Group have been making them available in the mainstream. But the challenge remains in finding products that taste

Introduction

good to you, so I've included the following list to help you understand the options.

Milk

Milk can be substituted by soy milk, which comes plain and unsweetened or flavored (vanilla or chocolate). Make sure you use plain soy milk when cooking unless the recipe specifies flavored. Rice milk and almond milk are also good substitutes if soy milk isn't to your liking. Both are a little sweeter than plain soy milk.

I like using West Soy and Westbrae lowfat soy milks (1 percent and 2 percent fat, plain or vanilla) because there is no predominant aftertaste that other brands of soy milk sometimes have. These are available in most food markets.

Pacific Foods Almond Milk is a great tasting milk substitute with a subtle almond flavor that's not overpowering and it's low in fat.

Check out my Vanilla-Soy Cappuccino (page 233) for a new dairy-free version of the coffee classic. (Many of the biggest coffee houses around the country are offering soy versions of my recipe, but making it for yourself is a real treat.)

If you're a die-hard milk drinker and have it in your cereal or drink it as a beverage and you want to wean yourself from it, start out by mixing the soy milk with your regular lowfat milk in a half-gallon container. Try 50 percent dairy milk mixed with 50 percent soy milk. Next time try to increase the percentage of the soy milk you add to the mixture. Eventually your taste buds will get used to the change and you will finally be free of this milk craving.

Make sure you shake the box of soy milk well before using it. You may notice a little sediment when you let the milk settle. Don't be concerned; this is normal. Soy milk is made from soybeans and filtered water, so it separates differently than regular milk.

Cheese

You may think a soy cheese may never taste as good to you as a fine imported cheese. If you cannot or do not eliminate cheese from

Totally
dairy-free
Cooking

your diet, then at least find a good soy cheese to use occasionally that simulates what you love about cheese without the health hazards of the added dairy. It might take a little experimenting to find a soy cheese that tastes good to you, but they do exist. I recommend using Soya Kaas or Lisanatti Soy-Sation. I think they taste the best and they melt better than other brands. Although they do include a small amount of casein, a lactose-free derivative of dairy that is used to aid in the melting, these soy cheeses have no cholesterol, are lactose free, include no hydrogenated oil and are low in saturated fat. There are also rice and almond cheeses. Again, everyone has a different palate, so try out these alternatives and select the ones you prefer.

Yogurt

Soy yogurt is an acquired taste if you're eating it plain but it's not if it's used in yogurt-based soups or in baking. The flavored soy yogurts are tasty enough to eat unadorned. Try White Wave Silk Dairyless or Nancy's Cultured Soy Yogurt.

Eggs

Contrary to popular belief and subliminally enhanced by grocery store dairy sections, eggs are not dairy (unless you've seen a cow lay an egg lately). They are an excellent source of protein containing all the necessary amino acids. If eggs are part of your diet, I recommend using free-range and/or organic eggs. It is important to use only these types of eggs because regular eggs from chicken farms are loaded with antibiotics and growth hormones, which are fed to chickens to produce larger and more meaty birds. To eat the meat from these birds is bad enough for you, but to eat the egg is even worse. A lower fat option is to use Eggology Liquid Egg Whites. They are pasteurized and come in a resealable plastic container. If eggs aren't part of your diet, or you are a vegan vegetarian I recommend using Ener-G Egg Replacer. It's a tapioca and potato starch combination that works beautifully for baking. Tofu (bean curd) has about the same consistency as eggs, and can have many different flavors depending on what you eat with it. You want to use a crumbled firm tofu for the best results when using it to simulate scrambled eggs.

Butter

The easiest substitute for butter is soy bean margarine, such as Shedd's Willow Run or Hain margarine. Vegetable oils, especially olive, safflower and canola oils are great substitutes (in nonbaked goods) as well. I like Spectrum Naturals Skillet spray and Cascadian Farms oils. When baking, substitute soy margarine equally whenever butter is called for in a recipe and if you want to cut down on fat, try mixing equal parts of soybean margarine with either tofu or applesauce.

Totally
daiRy-free
Cooking

All of these recipes can be served as hors d'oeuvres at a cocktail or dinner party or as a great way to start any meal. They're easy to make and are versatile if you have to prepare them in advance. Surprise your friends and family the next time they ask you to bring a snack for a gathering. See if they can tell there's no dairy in these recipes. Have fun with the presentation, too. All of these appetizers look as good as they taste.

CALORIES: 146

FAT: 10G

PROTEIN: 5.6G

CARBOHYDRATE: 11.3G

CHOLESTEROL: 0MG

SODIUM: 56MG

This is a wonderful dip to serve at any party. It's got a great nutty flavor. Even if you omit the walnuts the pâté will still taste delicious. Try spreading a thin layer on chicken or fish and broiling it with fresh bread crumbs sprinkled on top as a variation. (See page 94, Hummus–Crusted Salmon, for preparation.)

MAKES 8 SERVINGS **PREPARATION TIME: 30 MINUTES**

3 cups cremini mushrooms

1 tablespoon minced garlic

1 tablespoon minced shallots

1 tablespoon balsamic vinegar

Salt and freshly ground black pepper

1 cup green lentils

½ cup walnut pieces

½ cup chopped fresh basil

1 teaspoon ground bay leaves

1 tablespoon *umeboshi* plum paste, optional

2 teaspoons barley miso

3 tablespoons extra-virgin olive oil

Toasted pita wedges, rice crackers or Belgian endive, for serving

1. Preheat the oven to 350°F. Toss the mushrooms, garlic, shallots and vinegar in a mixing bowl. Season with salt and pepper to taste. Spread the mixture on a baking pan and roast for 15 minutes.

2. In a small saucepan, cook the lentils in 2 cups of water for 25 to 30 minutes, drain and reserve the cooking liquid.

3. Spread the walnuts on a baking pan and toast in the oven for 5 minutes. Set aside.

4. In a food processor combine the mushroom mixture, lentils, basil, bay leaves, *umeboshi* and miso. Drizzle in the olive oil and add the walnuts. Season with salt and pepper to taste. Serve with toasted pita wedges, rice crackers or endive.

NOTE: Add the reserved liquid from the lentils to thin out the mixture if it becomes too thick.

Totally
daiRY-free
cooking

CHILI-SEARED SHRIMP AND GUACAMOLE TORTILLA CRISPS

Place some baked tortilla chips on a platter and add a light dollop of guacamole right on the chips. Add the warm shrimp right out of the pan on top of the guacamole and you're ready to go. If you can't find the chili garlic paste, you can replace it with 1½ tablespoons of chili paste mixed with ½ tablespoon of minced garlic.

CALORIES: 99.2

FAT: 2.9G

PROTEIN: 13.8G

CARBOHYDRATE: 3.5G

CHOLESTEROL: 96MG

SODIUM: 550MG

MAKES 9 SERVINGS   PREPARATION TIME: 40 MINUTES, PLUS 2 TO 24 HOURS REFRIGERATION

1½ teaspoons coriander seeds

4 tablespoons tomato paste

1½ ounces tamari soy sauce

2 tablespoons rice wine (*mirin*)

2 tablespoons chili garlic paste

1 tablespoon fresh lemon juice

1 tablespoon olive oil

1½ tablespoons chili powder

36 medium shrimp, peeled and
   deveined

Six 8-inch flour or corn tortillas

Guacamole (page 161), for serving

1. Whisk all ingredients together except for the shrimp, chips, and guacamole. Add the shrimp, stir, and refrigerate a minimum of 2 hours, up to 24 hours.

2. Just before serving, preheat the oven to 350°F. Spray a non-stick baking tray with canola oil and cut your favorite flour or corn tortillas into wedges and bake for 3 to 4 minutes on each side or until crisp and set aside.

3. Heat a nonstick pan over medium heat, spray with canola oil spray, add the shrimp, and sear 1 minute on each side. Remove from the heat.

4. Serve the seared shrimp on top of the baked tortilla chips with a dollop of guacamole.

NOTES: Garnish with cilantro leaves and a dollop of Roasted Corn–Chipotle Salsa (page 169) or Mango, Tomato and Black Bean Salsa (page 153). A side of Mesclun Greens with Balsamic Mustard Vinaigrette (page 68) also makes a nice garnish.

APPETIZERS

✳ CHICKEN SATAY

This is almost guaranteed to be the hit of any cocktail party. I suggest preparing two to three skewers per person. You can make more if this is your only hors d'oeuvre. Try sprinkling toasted sesame seeds and/or sliced scallions over the Chicken Satay before serving. I like to make a few extra because these are even better the next day as a snack.

MAKES 16 TENDERS	PREPARATION TIME: 45 MINUTES

16 skewers, 5 to 7 inches

3 teaspoons tamari soy sauce

2 teaspoons rice wine (*mirin*)

½ teaspoon curry powder

1 teaspoon olive oil

1 pound boneless, skinless chicken breasts, cut into sixteen 1-ounce strips

Freshly ground black pepper

Ground coriander

Pinch of sea salt

½ cup almond milk, or soy milk

1 tablespoon canned unsweetened coconut milk

1 tablespoon unsweetened peanut butter

1 tablespoon pure maple syrup

1½ teaspoons arrowroot

Juice of ½ lime

½ teaspoon Thai chili paste, optional

1 tablespoon trimmed and thinly sliced scallions

1. If using wooden skewers, be sure to soak them in water in advance so they won't burn. In a mixing bowl, combine 2 teaspoons of the tamari, the wine, curry powder and olive oil. Add the chicken and season with pepper and coriander to taste and a pinch of sea salt. Marinate for at least 1 hour.

2. In a small pot over low heat, heat the almond milk for a minute. Whisk in the coconut milk, peanut butter, remaining 1 teaspoon tamari and the maple syrup.

3. Mix the arrowroot with 2 teaspoons of water in a separate bowl. Add to the peanut sauce, just as it starts to simmer. Stir constantly until the sauce thickens, 2 to 3 minutes. Add the lime juice and chili paste, if desired. Cover and keep in a warm place until ready to serve. Mix in the scallions just before serving.

Totally dairy-free cooking

4. Heat a nonstick grill pan or skillet over medium heat. Skewer the chicken pieces. Grill the chicken until cooked through, 2 to 3 minutes per side; check to see if they are cooked by inserting a paring knife in the center of the thickest strip. Serve with the warm peanut sauce.

When serving appetizers, decide whether you want finger food or dishes that require utensils. Choose your recipes accordingly.

✳ ROASTED EGGPLANT–WILD MUSHROOM CAKES

CALORIES: 150

FAT: 7.2G

PROTEIN: 10.2G

CARBOHYDRATE: 29.6G

CHOLESTEROL: 0MG

SODIUM: 1670MG

When preparing any of these appetizer cake recipes, try to find fresh finely grated bread crumbs at your local baker instead of using the commercially available ones since they tend to have a lot of dairy in them like Parmesan cheese or nonsolid milk products.

MAKES 6 SERVINGS (12 CAKES)	PREPARATION TIME: 1½ HOURS, PLUS 2 HOURS REFRIGERATION

One 1½-pound eggplant, peeled and cubed

4 teaspoons sea salt, plus additional for seasoning

2 tablespoons olive oil cooking spray (spray for 2 seconds)

2 tablespoons minced garlic

1 cup chopped onions

2 tablespoons balsamic vinegar

2 tablespoons dry cooking sherry, or sweet white wine

1 cup sliced cremini mushrooms

Freshly ground black pepper

¼ cup chopped fresh basil leaves

¼ cup minced fresh parsley

2 tablespoons soy Parmesan

2 tablespoons egg whites (from about 1 egg)

½ cup whole wheat bread crumbs

Roasted Tomato Vinaigrette (page 152), for serving

1. In a mixing bowl, toss the eggplant with the salt. Let sit for 20 to 30 minutes and rinse thoroughly to remove all bitterness from the eggplant.

2. Heat the olive oil in a large nonstick skillet over medium heat. Add the garlic and onions and cook, stirring, until the onions are translucent, about 3 minutes. Add the eggplant and cook, stirring, for 5 minutes more. Add the vinegar, sherry and mushrooms. Continue to cook until the eggplant is softened, 5 to 10 minutes more. Season with salt and pepper to taste. Mix in the basil and parsley and transfer into a mixing bowl.

3. When slightly cool put the mixture on a cutting board and fine chop with chef's knife. Put the mixture back in the bowl and fold in the Parmesan and egg whites.

4. Form the mixture into 12 balls, roll in the bread crumbs and

Totally dairy-free cooking

flatten slightly to form cakes. Place on a baking tray and refrigerate at least 2 hours before cooking.

5. Preheat the oven to 350°F. Spray a nonstick skillet with canola oil spray and heat over medium. Add the cakes and cook until browned on the bottom, 3 to 4 minutes. Turn over and cook until browned on the other side, 3 to 4 minutes more. Place on a baking tray and bake for 5 to 7 minutes. Serve with Roasted Tomato Vinaigrette.

NOTE: For a cocktail party, make 24 small cakes instead of 12 appetizer-size cakes.

CALORIES: 103.2

FAT: 3.3G

PROTEIN: 9.6G

CARBOHYDRATE: 16.9G

CHOLESTEROL: 34MG

SODIUM: 141MG

There's lots of texture and flavor in these Southwestern cakes. Their unique flavor comes from the tahini (ground sesame seeds). For best results, make sure you prepare this recipe well in advance of cooking, because the cakes need time to set in the refrigerator.

MAKES 10 SERVINGS (10 CAKES)   **PREPARATION TIME: 1½ HOURS, PLUS 1 TO 2 HOURS REFRIGERATION**

8 ounces medium shrimp, peeled and deveined

1 lemon

½ teaspoon sea salt, plus additional for seasoning

1 teaspoon Ancho Chili Dry Rub (page 166), or Old Bay Seasoning or other spice mix

¼ teaspoon ground coriander

⅛ teaspoon freshly ground black pepper, plus additional for seasoning

2 tablespoons olive oil

1 teaspoon minced garlic

1 teaspoon minced shallots

1 cup fresh or frozen corn kernels

1 tablespoon tahini (sesame paste)

1 tablespoon tamari soy sauce

1 teaspoon Dijon mustard

1 tablespoon soft tofu

1 tablespoon egg whites

1 cup hand-chopped, cooked black beans

⅓ cup whole wheat bread crumbs

Any salsa from this book or Roasted Tomato Vinaigrette (page 152), for serving

1. Soak the shrimp in ice water with the juice of ½ lemon and the ½ teaspoon of the salt for 30 minutes. Drain and chop into small pieces. Toss with the Ancho Chili Dry Rub, coriander, ⅛ teaspoon of the pepper and 1 tablespoon of the olive oil. Marinate for 30 minutes.

2. In a nonstick skillet, heat the remaining 1 tablespoon olive oil over medium heat. Cook the garlic and shallots, stirring, until the shallots are translucent, about 3 minutes. Add the corn kernels and cook, stirring, for 5 minutes. Add 2 tablespoons of water, if necessary, to keep the corn from burning. Add the chopped shrimp and continue to cook, stirring, until the shrimp are cooked, 2 to 3 minutes. Set aside.

Totally dairy-free cooking

3. In a mixing bowl, combine the tahini, tamari, Dijon, tofu, egg whites, beans and shrimp/corn mixture. Mix well and season with salt and pepper to taste. Form into 10 balls and roll them in the whole wheat bread crumbs. Make into cakes and place on a tray. Refrigerate for 1 to 2 hours to set before cooking.

4. Preheat the oven to 350°F. Spray a nonstick skillet with canola oil spray. Heat over medium-low heat, and add the cakes. Cook until golden on the bottom, 3 minutes, then turn over and cook until golden on the other side, 3 minutes. Place the cakes on a baking sheet and finish cooking in the oven for 5 minutes. Serve with salsa or the Roasted Tomato Vinaigrette.

NOTES: For a cocktail party, make 20 small cakes instead of 10 appetizer-size cakes. For a sit-down dinner all of the cakes in this chapter are great with a side of Mesclun Greens with Balsamic Mustard Vinaigrette (page 68).

✳ LUMP CRAB CAKES

CALORIES: 78.2

FAT: 2.5G

PROTEIN: 12.1G

CARBOHYDRATE: 8.3G

CHOLESTEROL: 40MG

SODIUM: 246MG

This is a healthful version of a great American favorite. Try adding some fresh diced avocado to the salsa for a creamier texture.

MAKES 10 SERVINGS (10 CAKES)	PREPARATION TIME: 45 MINUTES, PLUS 2 HOURS REFRIGERATION

The crab cakes, shrimp cakes and eggplant cakes need time to set in the refrigerator. Allow 2 to 4 hours, especially since the recipes don't use a lot of binders like whole eggs. Freeze extra cakes and serve them as appetizers when you have unexpected company.

1 pound lump crabmeat

1 tablespoon mayonnaise, preferably eggless

1 teaspoon Dijon mustard

1 teaspoon grated horseradish

2 tablespoons egg whites (from about 1 egg)

1 teaspoon Worcestershire sauce

1 tablespoon fresh lemon juice

¼ cup minced red bell peppers

½ teaspoon Old Bay Seasoning

2 tablespoons trimmed and thinly sliced scallions

1 tablespoon minced fresh parsley

1 teaspoon finely chopped fresh cilantro

½ teaspoon hot sauce, optional

1 teaspoon arrowroot

1 tablespoon plain soy milk

Sea salt and freshly ground black pepper

⅓ cup whole wheat bread crumbs

Lemon wedges and Three-Pepper Salsa (page 170), for serving

1. Clean and discard all shell fragments in the crabmeat. Set aside.

2. In a mixing bowl, whisk together all the remaining ingredients except for the bread crumbs and serving ingredients. Gently fold in the cleaned crabmeat. Form into 10 balls and roll in a small mixing bowl with the bread crumbs. Form into cakes and place on a sheet pan or tray. Refrigerate for at least 2 hours before cooking to set.

3. Preheat the oven to 350°F. Spray a nonstick skillet with canola oil spray. Heat the pan and cook the cakes until light brown, 2 to 3 minutes per side. Finish cooking on a baking tray in the oven for 5 to 7 minutes.

4. Serve with lemon wedges and Three-Pepper Salsa.

NOTE: For a cocktail party, make 20 small cakes instead of 10 appetizer-size cakes.

Totally dairy-free Cooking

✳ STEAMED YUKON POTATO AND BROCCOLI DUMPLINGS

Everyone loves dumplings and these won't disappoint anyone with the incredible combination of flavors. Even kids who refuse to eat their broccoli will enjoy these. Yukon potatoes give these dumplings an extra rich creamy flavor but you can substitute Idaho or red potatoes if you're in a pinch.

CALORIES: 35.9

FAT: 0.5G

PROTEIN: 1.2G

CARBOHYDRATE: 6.7G

CHOLESTEROL: 1MG

SODIUM: 293MG

MAKES 12 SERVINGS (36 DUMPLINGS)   **PREPARATION TIME: 1 HOUR**

1 teaspoon sea salt, plus additional
   for seasoning
1 pound Yukon Gold potatoes,
   scrubbed and diced
½ cup broccoli florets
½ cup whole spinach leaves
1 teaspoon red miso

¼ cup plain, lowfat soy milk
1 tablespoon soy margarine
Freshly ground black pepper
36 round wonton wrappers
Roasted Tomato and White Truffle
   Coulis (page 144), for serving

1. In a medium saucepan, bring 2 quarts of water with 1 teaspoon of sea salt to a boil. Add the potatoes and boil for 15 minutes, or until cooked through. Drain and set aside.

2. Bring another pot of water to a boil and blanch the broccoli florets and spinach leaves for 2 minutes. Drain and chill in ice water to keep their vibrant color.

3. In a mixing bowl, mash the potatoes with a fork. Finely chop the broccoli florets and spinach leaves and combine with the potatoes. Add the miso, soy milk, margarine, and salt and pepper to taste.

4. Place a wonton wrapper on a clean surface. Pat water around the edges. Place a teaspoon of the potato mixture in the center and fold over. Press firmly to seal. Use a fork to pinch the ends together forming half moon shaped dumplings. Repeat with the remaining dumplings. Keep refrigerated until needed.

5. To cook, place the cold dumplings in boiling water for 3 minutes. Drain and serve with Roasted Tomato and White Truffle Coulis.

APPETIZERS

✳ PAN-SEARED BLACK BEAN DUMPLINGS

CALORIES: 226.3

FAT: 8.2G

PROTEIN: 9.4G

CARBOHYDRATE: 29G

CHOLESTEROL: 2MG

SODIUM: 538MG

Marilu Henner's kids love these so much she featured them in her bestselling book, *Marilu Henner's Total Health Makeover*. If you can't find the chili garlic paste, you can replace it with 2 teaspoons of Thai chili paste and 1 teaspoon of chopped garlic. These can also be steamed for a more traditional presentation.

MAKES 4 SERVINGS (12 DUMPLINGS)   **PREPARATION TIME: 45 MINUTES**

1 cup canned or cooked, drained and mashed black beans

¼ cup tahini (sesame paste)

2 tablespoons trimmed and thinly sliced scallions

1 tablespoon tamari soy sauce

1 tablespoon rice wine (*mirin*)

½ teaspoon rice wine vinegar

½ teaspoon *ponzu* sauce (Japanese unsweetened citrus juice), or fresh lime juice

1 tablespoon chili garlic paste

12 round wonton wrappers

Red Miso–Mango Dipping Sauce (page 150), for serving

1. In a mixing bowl, blend all the ingredients together except for the wonton wrappers and dipping sauce.

2. Lay out the wrappers on a flat clean surface. Add approximately 1 teaspoon of mixture in the center of each skin. Brush a light coating of water around the edges of the skins and fold over to form a half moon. Repeat with the remaining wrappers and filling. Seal tightly with your fingers or use a fork to pinch the ends together. Refrigerate until ready to use.

3. Preheat the oven to 350°F. Spray a nonstick skillet with canola oil spray, set over medium heat, and cook 6 dumplings at a time. Brown each side 2 to 3 minutes. Finish cooking on a baking sheet in the oven for 5 minutes to warm the centers. Serve with Red Miso–Mango Dipping Sauce.

Totally
dairy-free
cooking

✳ LOBSTER, MANGO, AVOCADO AND ASPARAGUS SPRING ROLLS

Well worth the cost, these can be made in advance and served up when your guests arrive. Use a damp cloth covering to keep them moist until you're ready to serve. Refrigerate them if you are making them more than one hour in advance. You can use Seared Asian Tofu (page 184) in place of the lobster if you want to keep the spring roll completely vegetarian. Poached chicken or shrimp will also do very nicely.

CALORIES: 278.2

FAT: 7.1G

PROTEIN: 15.5G

CARBOHYDRATE: 37.5G

CHOLESTEROL: 36MG

SODIUM: 527MG

MAKES 2 SERVINGS　　　　　　　**PREPARATION TIME: 15 MINUTES**

2 medium asparagus, blanched in
　　simmering water for 1 minute, and
　　split lengthwise

4 thin slices mango

4 thin slices avocado

1 teaspoon extra-virgin olive oil

1 teaspoon fresh lemon juice

½ teaspoon minced fresh cilantro

Sea salt and freshly ground black
　　pepper

Two 8-inch rice flour skins

2 teaspoons Miso Wasabi Coulis
　　(page 149), or 1 teaspoon spicy
　　prepared mustard plus 1 teaspoon
　　eggless mayonnaise

½ cup cooked lobster meat

1. In a small bowl, toss the asparagus, mango, avocado, olive oil, lemon juice, cilantro and salt and pepper to taste.

2. Fill a medium pot with 3 inches of water and bring to a boil. Carefully place the rice flour skins in the water for 10 seconds. Remove and spread out on a plate.

3. Spread half of the Miso Wasabi Coulis in the center of each skin. Put in 2 pieces each of asparagus, mango and avocado on each skin. Top with half the lobster meat. Fold in the sides and roll like a burrito. Serve immediately or store in the refrigerator with a damp towel cover to keep moist. Cut each piece into 3 sections and serve sitting up on its side like sushi with the dipping sauce.

APPETIZERS

CALORIES: 243.9

FAT: 10.4G

PROTEIN: 13.8G

CARBOHYDRATE: 24.8G

CHOLESTEROL: 13MG

SODIUM: 484MG

A quesadilla with a crispy exterior, succulent melted cheese and lobster on the inside? How can you go wrong? I suggest serving these only when entertaining a small group. People gobble them up so quickly, you'll surely run out, leaving your guests begging for more. For a beautiful presentation, serve three wedges of the quesadilla arranged around a chopped salad, with Roasted Corn–Chipotle Salsa (page 169) or Tofu Sour Cream (page 163) on the side. You can substitute shrimp or crab equally for the lobster.

MAKES 2 SERVINGS   **PREPARATION TIME: 20 MINUTES**

Use one of the salads in this book as a garnish along with the appetizers to make a more complete dish and a better presentation.

1 teaspoon olive oil

¼ cup chopped fresh or frozen corn kernels

⅛ teaspoon ground coriander

⅛ teaspoon ground cumin

⅛ teaspoon chili powder

Sea salt and freshly ground black pepper

Two 8-inch whole grain flour tortillas

¼ cup cooked and diced lobster meat

1 tablespoon trimmed and thinly sliced scallions

¼ cup grated soy jalapeño cheese

1. Heat a small nonstick skillet with the olive oil and cook the corn, stirring, for 5 minutes. Add 1 tablespoon of water if the pan gets dry. Add the coriander, cumin, and chili powder and season with salt and black pepper to taste. Set aside.

2. In a medium nonstick skillet, place 1 tortilla on the bottom. Evenly distribute the corn, lobster, scallions, and cheese on the tortilla. Place the second tortilla on top and cook until golden on the bottom, 2 to 3 minutes. Turn the quesadilla over and cook until golden on the other side, 2 to 3 minutes more, or until the cheese melts. Cut into 6 pieces and serve immediately.

Totally dairy-free cooking

My mother is the soup queen. When I was a kid, she would make a big pot of a different soup every week. Watching her in the kitchen as I was growing up inspired me to get creative with my own soups. Specialty soup shops are becoming one of the fastest growing trends in food service. Making large batches of soup is an easy and economical way to feed any gathering, large or small. Some hearty soups can even be considered a complete meal. Every recipe in this chapter is a lowfat, healthful and delicious meal. Here's a free "stock" tip for you—freeze leftovers and you'll always have a delicious warm meal on those extra cold winter days. Hint: When you freeze your leftover stocks, try using ice cube trays. Place the trays inside a zip-top freezer bag and store it in your freezer. This little trick comes in handy whenever I need a small amount of stock for a specific recipe. I simply pop a cube or two out and use it as needed.

✳ ROASTED CHICKEN STOCK

Chicken soup can sometimes be deceiving because what usually gives it that wonderful full flavor is the fat from the chicken skin. When making this recipe, take the time to trim all the fat away from the chicken carcass. The roasting of the chicken dries up any excess fat and gives this a unique flavor that will be present in all of the soups and sauces you use it in.

MAKES 6 CUPS	PREPARATION TIME: 2 HOURS

2 chicken carcasses, trimmed of all fat

2 ribs celery, chopped

1 medium onion, chopped

1 head garlic, cut in half

1 large carrot, chopped

1 cup dry cooking sherry

1. Preheat the oven to 350°F. Place the chicken carcasses in a roasting pan and roast for 30 minutes, turning several times. Add the celery, onion, garlic and carrot to the roasting pan and roast 30 minutes more.

2. In a medium stockpot, add 10 cups of water and the roasted bones and vegetables. Bring to a boil, then reduce the heat and simmer for about 1 hour.

3. Drain the roasting pan of any excess fat, then place the roasting pan on top of the stove over medium heat. Add the sherry to deglaze the pan and scrape the drippings from the bottom of the pan. Add the pan drippings to the simmering stock.

4. After an additional hour, strain the stock through a fine-mesh strainer or cheesecloth, refrigerate for up to 5 days or freeze within 2 days until needed.

Totally
dairy-free
Cooking

✳ ASIAN CHICKEN SOUP

This soup's Asian flavor is light but very tasty. I'm always looking for ways to utilize every ingredient and not waste anything. Save the bones to use in Roasted Chicken Stock (page 40).

CALORIES: 234

FAT: 6.5G

PROTEIN: 31G

CARBOHYDRATE: 12G

CHOLESTEROL: 116MG

SODIUM: 399MG

MAKES 4 SERVINGS   **PREPARATION TIME: 15 MINUTES**

2 cups Roasted Chicken Stock
    (page 40)
Two ¼-inch pieces fresh ginger
2 skinless chicken thighs
2 skinless chicken legs
1 tablespoon tamari soy sauce
1 tablespoon rice wine (*mirin*)
1 cup diced daikon radishes
1 small red or yellow bell pepper,
    julienned

½ cup thinly sliced shiitake
    mushrooms
1 baby bok choy, sliced, or napa
    cabbage
½ cup trimmed and thinly sliced
    scallions
½ teaspoon sesame oil
½ teaspoon red pepper flakes

1. Place the chicken stock and 2 cups of water in 2-quart stockpot and bring to a boil. Add the ginger, chicken thighs and legs, tamari and wine. Bring back to a boil, then reduce the heat and simmer for 10 minutes.

2. Add the daikon and continue to simmer for an additional 10 minutes. Add the bell pepper and mushrooms and simmer for 5 more minutes. Add the bok choy, scallions, sesame oil and red pepper flakes, and cook for 1 minute.

3. Remove the chicken from the soup and pull the meat from bones. Chop the meat and return to the soup. Remove the ginger pieces from the soup and discard, and serve.

NOTES: Chicken breast can be used instead of legs and thighs. Poach whole chicken breast for 12 to 15 minutes and remove from the soup. Dice and return to the soup just before serving.

> Don't boil your stocks to try to make them cook faster. This will make them cloudy and the taste will suffer. It's worth taking the extra time to make stocks right. Remember, a good stock makes a great soup and adds extra flavor to any dish you use it in.

soups
and
stocks

✳ CHICKEN SOUP WITH MUSHROOMS AND PARSNIPS

CALORIES: 189.9

FAT: 5.9G

PROTEIN: 12.3G

CARBOHYDRATE: 15.3G

CHOLESTEROL: 44MG

SODIUM: 56MG

The gingerlike flavor from the carrotlike parsnips is the secret to this fantastic soup. This has become known as "Louie's penicillin."

MAKES 4 SERVINGS　　　　　　　　　**PREPARATION TIME: 45 MINUTES**

1 tablespoon olive oil

1 teaspoon minced garlic

½ cup chopped onions

½ cup diced carrots

½ cup chopped parsnips

½ cup dry cooking sherry

2 skinless chicken legs

2 skinless chicken thighs

4 cups Roasted Chicken Stock
  (page 40)

½ cup thinly sliced shiitake
  mushrooms

Sea salt and freshly ground black
  pepper

1. In a medium stockpot, heat the olive oil over medium heat. Add the garlic and onions and cook, stirring, until the onions are translucent, about 3 minutes. Add the carrots and parsnips and continue to cook, stirring, for 5 minutes.

2. Add the sherry and simmer until the liquid is reduced by half, 2 to 3 minutes. Add the chicken legs and thighs and stock and simmer for 30 minutes.

3. Remove the chicken from the soup and pull the meat off the bones. Chop the meat and add back to the soup with the shiitake mushrooms and simmer for 5 minutes. Season with salt and pepper to taste, and serve.

Totally dairy-free cooking

Take the extra time to trim all the fat from the duck bones. This will significantly reduce the fat content of the stock. Remember to use any unused portions of your duck for the other recipes in this book.

PER CUP	
CALORIES: 75	
FAT: 2G	
PROTEIN: 6G	
CARBOHYDRATE: 7.5G	
CHOLESTEROL: 29MG	
SODIUM: 92MG	

MAKES 5 CUPS	PREPARATION TIME: 2½ HOURS

1 whole duck carcass, all fat removed

1 large carrot, chopped

1 medium onion, chopped

1 medium parsnip, chopped

2 ribs celery, chopped

1 shallot, halved

1 cup red wine, such as cabernet or merlot

10 whole black peppercorns

1. Preheat the oven to 375°F. Place the duck carcass in a roasting pan and roast for 30 minutes. Add all the vegetables to the roasting pan and roast an additional 30 minutes.

2. Transfer the carcass and vegetables to a medium stockpot and add 12 cups of water and the peppercorns. Bring to a boil, reduce the heat, and simmer for 1½ hours.

3. Drain the roasting pan of any excess fat, then place the roasting pan on top of the stove over medium heat. Add the wine to deglaze the pan and scrape the drippings from the bottom of the pan. Add the pan drippings to the simmering stock.

4. Strain the stock through a fine-mesh strainer or cheesecloth and reserve in the refrigerator, for 3 to 4 days, for later use. You can freeze the stock for up to 90 days.

Soups and Stocks

✳ DUCK, CELERY ROOT AND ENOKI MUSHROOM SOUP

CALORIES: 152.3

FAT: 5.4G

PROTEIN: 11.4G

CARBOHYDRATE: 11.4G

CHOLESTEROL: 44MG

SODIUM: 127MG

The red wine and the duck stock give this brothy soup its rich full flavor. For a lighter version, try using chicken stock and chicken meat. Serve in a large bowl with cooked small pasta shells for a simple and complete meal in a bowl.

MAKES 8 SERVINGS   **PREPARATION TIME: 45 MINUTES**

1 tablespoon olive oil

1 tablespoon minced shallots

½ cup chopped onions

1 cup julienned leeks

¾ cup dry red wine, such as cabernet
   or merlot

1 cup chopped celery root

1 cup chopped carrots

5 cups Duck Stock (page 43)

8 to 10 ounces skinless duck
   leg/thigh meat on the bone

1 cup chopped red bell peppers

3 ounces enoki mushrooms (about
   ½ cup)

2 cups tightly-packed, julienned
   spinach leaves

Sea salt and freshly ground black
   pepper

Trimmed and sliced scallions, for
   serving

1. Heat olive oil in a medium stockpot over medium heat. Add the shallots, onions and leeks and cook, stirring, until the onions are translucent, about 5 minutes. Add the wine and simmer until the liquid is reduced by half.

2. Add the celery root, carrots, duck stock and duck legs and simmer for 20 minutes more. Add the red peppers, mushrooms and spinach and cook for 5 minutes.

3. Remove the duck legs and pull the meat from the bone. Chop the meat and return it to the soup. Season with salt and pepper to taste. Serve with sliced scallions.

Totally
dairy-free
Cooking

✳ VEGETABLE STOCK

Commercial vegetable stocks are easily found in any supermarket, but spending the time to create your own stock is well worth the time and effort. It's healthier and more pure in flavor than the store-bought version.

PER 1 CUP
CALORIES: 109.1
FAT: 3.2G
PROTEIN: 3.8G
CARBOHYDRATE: 20.8G
CHOLESTEROL: 0MG
SODIUM: 55MG

MAKE 6 CUPS   **PREPARATION TIME: 1 HOUR AND 50 MINUTES**

2 medium onions, quartered and unpeeled

2 medium carrots, sliced 1 inch thick

5 celery ribs, sliced 1 inch thick

1 medium bell pepper, quartered and seeded

2 cups mushroom stems and pieces (optional)

3 garlic cloves

1 tablespoon olive oil

½ bunch parsley

10 peppercorns

2 bay leaves

3 sprigs fresh thyme

1. Preheat the oven to 400°F. Toss all the vegetables, except the mushroom pieces, and the garlic in 1 tablespoon olive oil. Place in a roasting pan and roast for 30 to 40 minutes. (Place the mushroom pieces in the roasting pan for the last 15 minutes.) Add ½ cup of water if the vegetables are beginning to stick to the bottom of the pan.

2. Place the vegetables in a 4-quart stockpot. Scrape the bottom of the roasting pan into the pot and add 2 quarts of water. Add the parsley, peppercorns, bay leaves and thyme to the stockpot. Bring to a boil and reduce to a simmer for 1 hour. Strain through a fine-mesh strainer or cheesecloth. The stock can be stored in the refrigerator for up to 5 days.

soups
and
stocks

✳ 45

✳ BARLEY MISO BROTH WITH TOFU AND VEGETABLES

CALORIES: 102.6

FAT: 3.5G

PROTEIN: 8.4G

CARBOHYDRATE: 12.6G

CHOLESTEROL: 0MG

SODIUM: 705MG

Miso soup is known for its unique healing quality. The lighter barley miso in this recipe gives a clean, refreshing flavor to this classic miso soup. Miso should never be brought to a boil because boiling will destroy the beneficial cultures that make this soup so healthful.

MAKES 4 SERVINGS   **PREPARATION TIME: 30 MINUTES**

One 5-inch piece Japanese *kombu* (kelp)

6 medium shiitake mushrooms, cleaned and sliced

6 medium cremini mushrooms, cleaned and sliced

½ cup julienned carrots

½ cup sliced bok choy

2 tablespoons tamari soy sauce

1 sheet *nori* (seaweed)

¼ pound diced firm tofu

4 scallions, trimmed and thinly sliced

2½ tablespoons barley miso

1. Preheat the oven to 350°F. Heat 1 quart of water to a boil in a small stockpot. Add the *kombu* and cook for 10 minutes. Lower the head, add the vegetables and tamari, and simmer for 2 to 3 minutes.

2. Toast the *nori* in the oven for 3 to 5 minutes, until crispy. Slice the toasted *nori* into thin, matchlike strips.

3. Remove the pot from the heat and sprinkle in the tofu, scallions and *nori*. Mix in the miso thoroughly with a wooden spoon and serve immediately. Gently warm the next day if you have leftovers.

Totally dairy-free Cooking

✳ ROASTED KABOCHA SQUASH SOUP

Kabocha is similar to butternut squash. It has a little deeper flavor but you can substitute butternut squash if you can't find it. This incredible soup has been on the menu at Josie's and Josephina's since the day we opened, and has been featured in numerous publications throughout the country and as far away as Japan. Refrigerate it overnight, partially uncovered, for optimum flavor. Reheat to a simmer before serving.

CALORIES: 143

FAT: 3.5G

PROTEIN: 3.5G

CARBOHYDRATE: 22.2G

CHOLESTEROL: 0MG

SODIUM: 33MG

MAKES 8 SERVINGS   PREPARATION TIME: 2 HOURS

1 whole *kabocha* or butternut squash, halved and seeded

1 tablespoon honey

¼ teaspoon ground cinnamon

¼ teaspoon ground allspice

¼ teaspoon ground nutmeg

1 medium sweet potato, scrubbed

1 tablespoon plus 1 teaspoon olive oil

2 cups chopped yellow onions

1 tablespoon minced garlic

1 cup chopped celery

1 cup dry white wine

4 cups Vegetable Stock (page 45) or water

2 cups plain, lowfat soy milk

Sea salt and freshly ground white pepper

Toasted pumpkin seeds, optional

An electric handheld blender is the key to making simple purees and is a lot easier to clean than a food processor or drink blender.

1. Preheat the oven to 350°F. Rub the 2 halves (meat side only) of the squash with the honey, cinnamon, allspice and nutmeg. Rub the whole sweet potato with 1 teaspoon of the olive oil. Place the squash and sweet potato in a roasting pan or baking dish and roast for 1 hour. Remove from the oven and when cooled, scoop the meat out of the squash. Peel and coarsely chop the sweet potato. Set aside.

2. In medium stockpot, heat the remaining 1 tablespoon of olive oil over medium heat. Add the onions, garlic and celery and cook, stirring, until softened, 5 to 7 minutes. Add the wine and simmer for 10 minutes. Add the stock and simmer for 15 minutes more.

3. Add the squash meat and sweet potatoes to the pot and simmer for 10 minutes, or until the sweet potatoes are tender. Remove from the heat and puree the mixture with an electric handheld blender, or in a food processor. Strain the soup through a fine-mesh strainer for a smoother texture, season and serve. Garnish with toasted pumpkin seeds, if you wish.

soups and stocks

✳ NEW ENGLAND–STYLE CLAM CHOWDER

CALORIES: 206.1

FAT: 7.1G

PROTEIN: 10.6G

CARBOHYDRATE: 26.2G

CHOLESTEROL: 13MG

SODIUM: 211MG

I suggest making your own clam stock and using fresh clams bought from your local seafood store when making this soup. But if you don't have the time, buy a commercially canned clam broth, available at all food markets. Make sure there is no MSG (monosodium glutamate) in the ingredients. You can usually find fresh chopped or minced clams at most seafood stores. When I came to New York from San Francisco and opened my first restaurant, Coastal, my recipe for New England Clam Chowder won the *New York Times*'s "Best of the Best" in the chowder category two years in a row. I felt challenged to try to reproduce the gorgeous flavor of that dairy laden version minus the dairy and this recipe is a real winner. My secret ingredient is the spicy chicken sausage that replaces the traditional slab bacon.

MAKES 12 SERVINGS	PREPARATION TIME: 1½ HOURS

1 tablespoon olive oil

3 cloves garlic, sliced

1 large shallot, sliced

One 4-ounce precooked, spicy chicken sausage, sliced

2 cups canned whole plum tomatoes

2 tablespoons Worcestershire sauce

1 cup diced bell peppers

1 cup diced carrots

1 cup diced onions

1 cup diced celery

1 cup fresh or frozen corn kernels

6 cups Clam Stock (page 50) or commercial clam juice (no MSG)

1¼ cups chopped fresh clams

½ teaspoon chopped fresh thyme

½ teaspoon chopped fresh oregano

3 cups peeled and diced Idaho potatoes

½ cup chopped fresh parsley

¼ cup trimmed and chopped scallions

2 teaspoons Old Bay Seasoning

Freshly ground black pepper

2 cups plain soy milk

4 tablespoons arrowroot

1. Heat the olive oil in a medium stockpot over medium-high heat. Add the garlic and shallots and cook, stirring, until the shallots are golden, 1 to 2 minutes. Add the sausage and cook, stirring, until

Totally dairy-free cooking

48 ✳

browned, about 5 minutes. Add the tomatoes and Worcestershire sauce and simmer 5 minutes. Puree the mixture with an electric handheld blender or in a food processor and return to the pot.

2. Add the bell peppers, carrots, onions, celery and corn and simmer 10 minutes. Add the clam juice, clams, thyme and oregano. Simmer 25 minutes more.

3. Add the potatoes, parsley and scallions. Simmer 15 minutes more, stirring frequently to avoid burning. Add the Old Bay Seasoning and black pepper to taste. Then whisk in the soy milk.

4. In a separate bowl, mix the arrowroot with ¼ cup water and add to the chowder and cook for an additional 3 to 4 minutes, then serve. Refrigerate for up to 5 days. Bring to a simmer when reheating.

Soups
and
Stocks

* 49

When you are finished making this stock, hand chop the whole clams and refrigerate them to use in the New England–Style Clam Chowder on page 48.

MAKES 6 CUPS   **PREPARATION TIME: 30 MINUTES**

2 dozen cherrystone clams, cleaned   1 large shallot, sliced

2 cups dry white wine   2 cloves garlic, sliced

1. In a medium stockpot, place the clams, wine, 1 cup of water, the shallots and garlic. Bring to a boil, then reduce the heat and simmer for 5 minutes, covered.

2. Remove any clams that are steamed open already and set aside in a bowl. Add 3 cups of water and simmer, covered, for 15 minutes more, removing the clams as they open. Strain the stock through a fine-mesh strainer or cheesecloth.

Totally dairy-free cooking

✳ LOBSTER STOCK

What do you do with all of those shells from your summer lobster boil? I rinse and freeze them for a rainy day when I want to make this special stock. Brandy gives it a smoky, full-bodied flavor.

PER CUP

CALORIES: 70

FAT: 0.6G

PROTEIN: 3.5G

CARBOHYDRATE: 3.3G

CHOLESTEROL: 57MG

SODIUM: 203MG

| MAKES 10 CUPS | PREPARATION TIME: 3½ HOURS |

Four 1¼-pound lobsters (if you don't already have the shells)

1 onion, chopped

2 carrots, chopped

2 ribs celery, chopped

1 cup brandy, or dry cooking sherry

1. If you don't already have the shells, cook the whole lobsters for 5 minutes in a large pot of boiling water. Drain and rinse under cold water. Remove the meat from the tails and claws and reserve the meat in the refrigerator for another use. If you have shells that you have frozen, be sure to rinse them under cold water before using.

2. Preheat the oven to 375°F. Place the shells in a roasting pan and roast for 30 minutes. Add the vegetables and roast for 30 minutes more. Transfer the shells and vegetables to a large stockpot.

3. Set the roasting pan on the stove top over medium heat and add the brandy to deglaze.

4. Add 1 gallon plus 2 cups of water and the pan drippings to the shells. Bring to a boil, then reduce the heat and simmer for 45 minutes to 1 hour.

5. Strain through a fine-mesh strainer or cheesecloth, return the stock to the pot, and simmer for 1½ hours more. Strain through a fine-mesh strainer or cheesecloth again. This stock can be stored for 3 to 4 days in the refrigerator or kept frozen for up to 90 days.

soups
and
stocks

CALORIES: 221

FAT: 2.9G

PROTEIN: 8.2G

CARBOHYDRATE: 18.6G

CHOLESTEROL: 25MG

SODIUM: 120MG

This soup will go head-to-head against any cream-based bisque. I believe in using fish stocks in fish-based soups and sauces to keep the flavor of the soup pure. Many chefs replace fish stock with chicken stock for its stronger flavor. That is not our philosophy at Josie's. If you're going to replace the lobster stock in this recipe, I suggest using a vegetable stock, or even a vegetable bouillon. If you want a smoother textured soup, strain it through a fine-mesh strainer after you puree it, but this will reduce your yield.

MAKES 10 SERVINGS **PREPARATION TIME: 3 HOURS**

2 medium sweet potatoes

1 tablespoon olive oil

3 cups chopped onions

1 cup chopped carrots

1 cup chopped celery

1 cup fresh or frozen corn kernels

1 cup dry white wine

1 cup brandy

10 cups Lobster Stock (page 51)

2 cups lowfat vanilla soy milk

Sea salt and freshly ground black
   pepper

Never completely cover a hot soup before storing it because the heat will have no place to escape to and the soup will spoil faster.

1. Preheat the oven to 350°F. Scrub the sweet potatoes to clean and place in a baking dish. Roast in the oven for 1 hour and 15 minutes. Remove from the oven and set aside.

2. Heat the olive oil in a medium stockpot over medium heat. Add the onions and cook, stirring, until translucent, about 5 minutes. Add the carrots, celery and corn, and continue to cook, stirring, for 5 minutes more.

3. Add the wine and brandy and simmer until the liquid is reduced by half, 4 to 5 minutes. Add the lobster stock and bring to a boil. Reduce the heat and simmer for 20 minutes.

4. Peel the cooled sweet potatoes and chop into large pieces (about 5 cups). Add to the soup.

5. Puree the soup with an electric handheld blender or in a food processor. While blending, add the soy milk slowly. Season with salt and pepper to taste and serve.

Totally
dairy-free
cooking

✳ TOMATO AND CHICKPEA BISQUE

Your family will think you spent hours in the kitchen when you serve them this soup but your secret is safe with me. This intensely flavored soup is quick and easy to make. Strain through a fine-mesh strainer for a more refined texture. For a crunchy garnish, try using croutons with a dollop of pesto.

CALORIES: 126.2

FAT: 3.8G

PROTEIN: 5.5G

CARBOHYDRATE: 19.5G

CHOLESTEROL: 0MG

SODIUM: 153MG

MAKES 8 SERVINGS   **PREPARATION TIME: 20 MINUTES**

1 tablespoon olive oil

1 tablespoon minced garlic

1 tablespoon minced shallots

1 cup chopped onions

4 cups canned whole plum tomatoes, drained

½ cup minced fresh basil

1 teaspoon minced fresh thyme, or ½ teaspoon dried

1 teaspoon minced fresh oregano

1 teaspoon red pepper flakes, optional

1½ cups (15-ounce can) canned, drained chickpeas

2 cups plain soy milk

Sea salt and freshly ground black pepper

1. In a medium stockpot, heat the olive oil over medium heat. Add the garlic and shallots and cook, stirring, until golden, about 2 minutes. Add the onions and cook, stirring, until translucent, about 5 minutes. Add the tomatoes and bring to a simmer. Add the basil, thyme, oregano and pepper flakes, if desired, and simmer for 5 to 7 minutes. Add the chickpeas and soy milk and season with salt and pepper to taste.

2. Puree the soup using an electric handheld blender or blend in a food processor, and serve.

SOUPS
and
Stocks

✳ TOMATO AND WHITE BEAN SOUP WITH ROASTED VEGETABLES

CALORIES: 142.1

FAT: 5.5G

PROTEIN: 5.7G

CARBOHYDRATE: 21.7G

CHOLESTEROL: 0MG

SODIUM: 17MG

This is an adaptation of Grandma Josephina's famous minestrone soup. It's a classic and was one of my favorites when I was a kid.

MAKES 6 SERVINGS   PREPARATION TIME: 45 MINUTES

2 tablespoons olive oil

6 cloves garlic, minced

One 14½-ounce can whole plum
    tomatoes, drained

20 fresh basil leaves

5 fresh sage leaves

1⅔ cups Vegetable Stock (page 45)
    or water

⅓ cup diced carrots

⅓ cup diced eggplant

⅓ cup diced celery

⅓ cup diced parsnips

⅓ cup diced onions

Salt and freshly ground black pepper

One 15-ounce can white beans,
    drained and rinsed

When buying a water filter, make sure it filters out chemicals, pesticides, heavy metals and parasites. A standard granular carbon filter will not filter out parasites, which are especially prevalent in areas with surface water sources, i.e., reservoirs.

1. In a medium stockpot, heat 1 tablespoon of olive oil over medium heat, add the garlic, and cook, stirring, until golden, about 1 minute. Add the tomatoes, 14 of the basil leaves and the sage leaves. Cook for 7 minutes, then add the vegetable stock. Bring to a boil and reduce the heat to a simmer for 15 minutes.

2. Meanwhile, preheat the oven to 350°F. Toss all the vegetables with the remaining 1 tablespoon olive oil. Season with salt and pepper to taste and place on a nonstick baking tray. Roast in the oven for 15 minutes, or until the vegetables are tender.

3. Add the beans to the soup and stir. Remove from the heat and puree soup with an electric handheld blender or in a food processor. Season with salt and pepper to taste.

4. Add the roasted vegetables to the soup puree and stir over low heat. Serve, garnished with the remaining 6 basil leaves.

Totally
dairy-free
cooking

✳ PUREE OF WILD MUSHROOM SOUP WITH TARRAGON

This is one of the easiest soups you will ever make. It has great flavor and is lowfat, too. For a special treat, drizzle white truffle oil over the top just before serving.

CALORIES: 55.5

FAT: 0.5G

PROTEIN: 2.3G

CARBOHYDRATE: 11.5G

CHOLESTEROL: 0MG

SODIUM: 1068MG

MAKES 16 SERVINGS   **PREPARATION TIME: 1¼ HOURS**

2½ quarts vegetable stock or water

8 ounces cremini mushrooms, sliced

6 ounces shiitake mushrooms, sliced

8 ounces portobello mushrooms, sliced

2 pounds Idaho potatoes, peeled and chopped

2 tablespoons minced garlic

1 tablespoon minced shallots

2 tablespoons minced fresh tarragon

Sea salt and freshly ground black pepper

1 cup lowfat plain soy milk

Chopped fresh chives or chervil, for garnish

1. Heat the vegetable stock in a medium stockpot. Add the mushrooms, potatoes, garlic, shallots, and tarragon. Bring to a boil, then reduce the heat and simmer about 45 minutes, or until the potatoes are soft.

2. Puree the soup with an electric handheld blender or in a food processor. Season to taste with salt and pepper. Whisk in the soy milk and serve. Garnish with chives or chervil.

soups and stocks

✳ YELLOW AND GREEN SPLIT PEA SOUP

CALORIES: 264.4

FAT: 2.2G

PROTEIN: 16.9G

CARBOHYDRATE: 42.6G

CHOLESTEROL: 0MG

SODIUM: 339MG

Split pea soup usually calls for ham as one of the ingredients, but this recipe is so good, you won't miss the ham at all. Miso more than compensates for the ham flavor. The soup tastes best when it has been refrigerated at least 24 hours prior to serving to let the flavors develop. Croutons are the classic garnish, or try it with a sprinkle of minced fresh oregano, finely chopped, blanched carrots or Lightlife Fakin Bacon Bits on top for an added treat.

MAKES 14 SERVINGS	PREPARATION TIME: 1¼ HOURS , PLUS 1 HOUR RESTING TIME

1 tablespoon olive oil

1 tablespoon minced shallots

1 medium onion, chopped

1 cup chopped carrots

½ cup chopped celery

½ cup dry cooking sherry

½ cup dry white wine

1 pound yellow split peas

1 pound green split peas

12 cups Vegetable Stock (page 45)

2 teaspoons sea salt

1 teaspoon freshly ground black
    pepper

1 tablespoon light chickpea miso, or
    regular miso

1 cup plain soy milk

1. In a large stockpot, heat the olive oil over medium heat. Add the shallots and cook, stirring, until golden, about 2 minutes. Add the onions, carrots and celery and cook, stirring, until the vegetables are softened, about 10 minutes.

2. Add the sherry and wine and simmer until the liquid is reduced by half. Add both kinds of split peas and the stock. Bring to a boil, then reduce the heat and simmer for 30 to 40 minutes, until the peas are mushy.

3. Remove from the heat and puree the mixture with an electric handheld blender or blend in a food processor until smooth.

4. Add the salt, pepper, miso and soy milk. Continue to blend thoroughly. Transfer to a storage container and let sit for at least 1 hour to develop flavors. Reheat the soup to a simmer before serving.

Totally
daiRy-free
cooking

✳ CARROT AND GINGER PUREE

If you're a carrot juice fan, this satisfying and delicious soup is for you. This is also a good vegetarian stand-in for Grandma's chicken soup when you're sick or just feel like you need some good old-fashioned comfort food. The soup can also be strained through a fine-mesh strainer for a silky texture.

CALORIES: 86.7

FAT: 1.4G

PROTEIN: 2.1G

CARBOHYDRATE: 15.7G

CHOLESTEROL: 0MG

SODIUM: 46MG

MAKES 16 SERVINGS   **PREPARATION TIME: 1¼ HOURS**

1 tablespoon olive oil

3 tablespoons minced shallots

1 teaspoon minced garlic

2 tablespoons chopped fresh ginger

3 pounds carrots, peeled and
    chopped

2 cups cleaned and sliced leeks

2 cups chopped onions

2½ quarts Vegetable Stock
    (page 45) or water

1 teaspoon chopped fresh thyme, or
    ½ teaspoon dried

2 cups carrot juice

½ cup rice wine (mirin)

Sea salt

⅛ teaspoon freshly ground black
    pepper

1 cup lowfat, vanilla soy milk

1. Heat the olive oil in a medium stockpot over medium heat. Add the shallots, garlic and ginger and cook, stirring, until the shallots are golden, about 2 minutes. Add the carrots, leeks and onions and cook, stirring, for 10 minutes.

2. Add the vegetable stock and thyme. Simmer for 45 minutes or until the carrots are soft. Add the carrot juice and wine and bring to a boil. Remove from the heat.

3. Puree the soup using an electric handheld blender or in a food processor. Season with salt and black pepper. Whisk in the soy milk slowly.

soups
and
stocks

✳ PUREE OF BLACK BEAN SOUP WITH CHILI AND HERBS

CALORIES: 161.8

FAT: 0.9G

PROTEIN: 9.6G

CARBOHYDRATE: 29G

CHOLESTEROL: 0MG

SODIUM: 24MG

This is an incredible soup for people who love herbs and spices. It's got a real kick to it, so get ready for that one-two punch! Try garnishing with one of the salsa recipes for some extra zing. This soup is designed to be made in big batches and it freezes well.

MAKES 14 SERVINGS   PREPARATION TIME: 2 HOURS, PLUS OVERNIGHT BEAN SOAKING

8 cups dried black beans (almost 3¼ pounds)
2½ quarts Vegetable Stock (page 45) or water
2 tablespoons chopped fresh oregano or 1 tablespoon dried
1 tablespoon chopped fresh thyme
2 tablespoons minced shallots
1 tablespoon minced garlic
1½ cups finely chopped carrots
2 cups minced onions
1 cup finely chopped celery
5 tablespoons rice wine (*mirin*)

¼ teaspoon cayenne pepper
1½ teaspoons chili powder
1 teaspoon curry powder
1 teaspoon ground cumin
1 teaspoon paprika
1 teaspoon ground coriander
¼ teaspoon freshly ground black pepper
Sea salt
⅓ cup chopped fresh cilantro
Tofu Sour Cream (page 163) for garnish, optional

> Make soup in big batches so you can freeze the leftovers. The proper way to freeze soup is to bring it down to a temperature under 50°F, uncovered, in an ice bath or refrigerator. Tightly seal the soup in a plastic container and put it in the freezer. Don't forget to date and label the soup. Use it within 60 days for the best flavor.

1. Rinse the beans and soak them overnight in a pot with enough water to cover by 3 inches. Drain and rinse the beans the next day. Place in medium stockpot and add enough water to cover. Bring to a boil and simmer for 10 minutes. Reduce the heat and simmer for 50 minutes or until the beans are semisoft. Add water if necessary to keep the bottom from burning. Drain the beans and set aside.

2. Heat the vegetable stock in a medium stockpot. Add all the ingredients except for the black beans, salt, pepper, cilantro and garnish. Bring to a boil, then reduce the heat and simmer for 15 minutes. Add the beans, pepper and salt to taste. Continue to cook for 10 minutes. Remove from the heat and puree the mixture with an electric handheld blender or in a food processor.

3. Add the cilantro and serve with a dollop of Tofu Sour Cream, if desired.

Totally dairy-free Cooking

✳ GAZPACHO

This is a spiced version of the classic recipe. Try adding finely diced firm tofu for extra texture and protein.

CALORIES: 74.6

FAT: 3.5G

PROTEIN: 1.6G

CARBOHYDRATE: 10.7G

CHOLESTEROL: 0MG

SODIUM: 161MG

MAKES 8 SERVINGS   **PREPARATION TIME: 30 MINUTES, PLUS 2 HOURS REFRIGERATION**

2 tablespoons olive oil

1 tablespoon minced garlic

1 cup fresh or frozen (thawed) corn kernels

One 14½-ounce can whole plum tomatoes

12 ounces tomato juice

2 tablespoons freshly squeezed lemon juice

2 tablespoons peeled and grated horseradish

¼ cup julienned fresh basil

¼ cup minced fresh cilantro

2 tablespoons balsamic vinegar

Sea salt and freshly ground white pepper

Tabasco sauce

1 cup diced jicama

1 cup peeled and diced cucumber

¼ cup diced yellow bell peppers

¼ cup diced red bell peppers

1. In a small skillet over medium heat, heat the olive oil. Add the garlic and cook, stirring, until golden, about 1 minute. Add the corn kernels and cook, stirring, for 5 to 7 minutes more. Remove from the heat and set aside.

2. In a large bowl, combine the tomatoes with their liquid, tomato juice, lemon juice, horseradish, basil, cilantro and vinegar. Season with salt, white pepper and Tabasco to taste. Add the cooked corn, jicama, cucumber and bell peppers. Mix well and adjust the seasonings. Refrigerate for at least 2 hours before serving.

soups and stocks

✳ SUMMER FRUIT SOUP

CALORIES: 117

FAT: 1.5G

PROTEIN: 2.5G

CARBOHYDRATE: 25.9G

CHOLESTEROL: 0MG

SODIUM: 127MG

This is a great start to any summer barbecue. It is also an excellent intermezzo. Leftovers can be used to make a healthful and delicious fruit smoothie the next day, too.

MAKES 6 SERVINGS   PREPARATION TIME: 20 MINUTES, PLUS SEVERAL HOURS TO CHILL

½ honeydew melon, peeled, seeded
    and diced
1 ripe mango, peeled and sliced
2 cups lowfat almond milk or soy milk
One 6-ounce container strawberry
    soy yogurt

¼ teaspoon sea salt
½ cup sliced strawberries
½ cup whole blueberries
2 tablespoons sliced mint leaves

1. In a food processor, add the honeydew and mango. Add the almond milk, yogurt and salt and puree until smooth. Refrigerate for several hours.

2. Serve the mixture in chilled shallow bowls, garnished with strawberry slices, blueberries and mint chiffonade.

Totally
dairy-free
Cooking

Buying quality lettuce is key in making any salad taste fresh and delicious. The prepackaged or prewashed lettuce sold in grocery stores is not your best choice. The processing of the lettuce removes all of the natural preservatives that keep it fresh. Invest in a salad spinner and wash lettuce as you need it. When buying lettuce, the deeper green the leaf, the higher the vitamin content. Try mixing different types of lettuce to give your salads a little extra zest.

All of the dressings in this chapter are creamy versions of your favorite salad dressings without the dairy. My customers at Josie's love our salads and dressings so much, they're always asking for the recipes. Now you will know our secrets, too! For a little adventure, use the dressings as marinades.

I often find that I enjoy a lighter meal, especially in spring and summer, but still want to get my protein. To make a salad into a main dish, top it with a piece of grilled fish or chicken.

✳ TABOULE

CALORIES: 182

FAT: 2.4G

PROTEIN: 6G

CARBOHYDRATE: 36.6G

CHOLESTEROL: 0MG

SODIUM: 279MG

This is great as a salad, a side dish or an appetizer for lunch or dinner. It's easy to make and can be prepared in advance. For a Mediterranean flair, it's also excellent served with hummus and crackers or pita crisps. Try it as filler for your favorite wrap sandwich or inside a pita.

MAKES 8 SERVINGS   PREPARATION TIME: 30 MINUTES, PLUS A FEW HOURS REFRIGERATION

½ cup cracked bulgur wheat

1 cup minced fresh parsley

¼ cup minced yellow onions

2 tablespoons fresh lemon juice (from about 1 lemon)

1 tablespoon extra-virgin olive oil

1 teaspoon minced garlic

½ teaspoon dried oregano

6 fresh basil leaves, julienned

1 teaspoon salt

¼ teaspoon freshly ground black pepper

1. In a medium pot, simmer the bulgur in 1¼ cups water for 15 minutes. Set aside in a bowl covered with plastic wrap. The bulgur will have swelled to 1½ cups.

2. In a separate bowl, mix together the remaining ingredients. Blend in the cooked bulgur when it is cool. Refrigerate for a few hours or overnight before serving.

Totally
daiRY-free
Cooking

✳ ALMOST CAESAR SALAD

A good Caesar salad is always a treat. This vegetarian version sneaks in a surprise taste, shredded seaweed, giving this salad its traditional anchovy taste without the fish. For a creamier version lower in fat, substitute ½ cup soft tofu for half of the oil.

CALORIES: 207.7

FAT: 21.2G

PROTEIN: 2.3G

CARBOHYDRATE: 3.7G

CHOLESTEROL: 0MG

SODIUM: 240MG

MAKES 8 SERVINGS   **PREPARATION TIME: 30 MINUTES**

¼ cup balsamic vinegar

6 tablespoons Dijon mustard

¼ cup rinsed and drained capers

1 tablespoon minced garlic

1 tablespoon minced shallots

¼ cup fresh lemon juice (from 1 to 2 lemons)

6 tablespoons extra-virgin olive oil

6 tablespoons canola oil

1 tablespoon minced fresh parsley

¼ cup shredded seaweed (agar), or julienned *nori* sheets

2 bunches romaine lettuce

Sea salt and freshly ground black pepper

2 tablespoons soy Parmesan

Wrap lettuce or mesclun greens in paper towels before you put it into a bag to remove any excess moisture. This prevents premature browning.

1. In a bowl using an electric handheld blender, puree the vinegar, mustard, capers, garlic, shallots and lemon juice. Slowly drizzle in the olive and canola oils. Mix in the parsley and seaweed by hand. Refrigerate. (The dressing will last in the refrigerator for up to 1 week in an airtight container.)

2. In a mixing bowl, tear the lettuce into bite-size pieces and season with salt and pepper to taste. Add the dressing and toss well. Serve on chilled plates with the Parmesan sprinkled on top.

SALads

✳ MESCLUN GREENS WITH RED WINE–MUSTARD VINAIGRETTE

CALORIES: 47.8

FAT: 0.8G

PROTEIN: 1.5G

CARBOHYDRATE: 9.8G

CHOLESTEROL: 0MG

SODIUM: 305MG

This is a pungent, spicy dressing that holds its flavor with the strong taste of mesclun lettuce. For an entrée salad, serve with grilled breast of chicken, grilled salmon or yellowfin tuna, or Seared Asian Tofu (page 184). Spoon a little Mango, Tomato and Black Bean Salsa (page 153) or Tomato Basil Concasse (page 151) on the fish for an exotic and refreshing light meal.

MAKES 12 SERVINGS (2¼ CUPS)	PREPARATION TIME: 20 MINUTES

When dressing your salads, always use a little less than you think you need, because you can always add more but you can't take any out.

10 tablespoons red wine vinegar

¼ cup tamari soy sauce

7 tablespoons fruit juice concentrate

1 teaspoon minced shallots

1 teaspoon minced garlic

¼ teaspoon sea salt

¼ cup Japanese *wasabi* mustard
    powder

3 ounces soft tofu

24 ounces mesclun

In a mixing bowl using an electric handheld blender, puree all of the ingredients except the mesclun, adding the tofu at the end.

NOTE: Use approximately 3 tablespoons vinaigrette with 2 ounces of mesclun greens for an average salad.

Totally dairy-free cooking

✳ SPINACH SALAD WITH ROASTED BEETS AND SEARED ASIAN TOFU

This is a meal in itself but it goes well as a side dish to liven up simple grilled fish or chicken. Try adding diced pear, apple or jicama for a crunchy treat or even peanuts or cashews for some extra protein.

CALORIES: 230

FAT: 10.5G

PROTEIN: 9.7G

CARBOHYDRATE: 30G

CHOLESTEROL: 0MG

SODIUM: 89MG

MAKES 4 SERVINGS　　　　　　　　　**PREPARATION TIME: 1½ HOURS**

1 medium beet

1 tablespoon canola oil, plus
　additional for coating beet

3 tablespoons rice wine vinegar

One 1½-inch piece fresh ginger,
　peeled and chopped

6 ounces whole spinach leaves,
　washed and spun dry

12 yellow cherry tomatoes, halved

1 cup diced Seared Asian Tofu (page
　184)

1 tablespoon extra-virgin olive oil

Sea salt and freshly ground black
　pepper

1. Preheat the oven to 350°F. Rub the beet skin with canola oil and roast for 1 hour. Cool the beet and peel the skin under running water. Dice and set aside.

2. In a small saucepan over medium heat, heat the vinegar to just below the boiling point, and pour over the ginger in a small bowl. After 15 minutes, strain the vinegar and set aside. Discard the ginger.

3. In a mixing bowl, combine the spinach, beet, tomatoes and tofu. Add 1 tablespoon canola oil, the olive oil and gingered vinegar. Mix thoroughly and season with salt and pepper to taste.

SALads

✳ 67

CALORIES: 140.8

FAT: 14G

PROTEIN: 0.6G

CARBOHYDRATE: 4.4G

CHOLESTEROL: 0MG

SODIUM: 166MG

This is the house vinaigrette at Josie's. I wouldn't call it my house dressing if it wasn't delicious. Mesclun is a mix of organic farmed baby lettuces available in most produce sections. For a creamier, lower-fat version, replace half the olive oil and half the canola oil with soft tofu and blend. For a refreshing herbal flavor add some basil, cilantro, parsley or chervil leaves to the mesclun mix. If you don't have walnut oil, you can substitute an equal amount of canola or olive oil.

MAKES 12 SERVINGS (2¼ CUPS)	PREPARATION TIME: 20 MINUTES

1 teaspoon minced garlic

¼ cup minced shallots

½ cup Dijon mustard

⅔ cup balsamic vinegar

1½ tablespoons honey

¼ teaspoon sea salt

⅛ teaspoon freshly ground black
    pepper

6 tablespoons extra-virgin olive oil

¼ cup canola oil

2 tablespoons walnut oil

1 tablespoon fresh minced parsley

24 ounces mesclun

In a mixing bowl, with an electric handheld mixer, puree the garlic, shallots, mustard, vinegar, honey, salt and pepper. While mixing, slowly add the 3 types of oil to form an emulsified dressing. Mix in the parsley by hand. Refrigerate for up to 2 weeks in a sealed airtight container.

NOTE: Use approximately 3 tablespoons of the vinaigrette with 2 ounces of mesclun greens for an average salad.

Totally dairy-free cooking

✳ CHOPPED VEGETABLE, TOFU AND ROMAINE SALAD

Who says Los Angeles has the best chopped salads? Not me. I suggest doubling this recipe, adding the oil and vinegar only to the part you are going to eat right away. You can eat this as a salad, or roll it into a tortilla wrap for a quick, satisfying vegetarian meal on the go.

CALORIES: 91.9

FAT: 7.2G

PROTEIN: 3.7G

CARBOHYDRATE: 5G

CHOLESTEROL: 0MG

SODIUM: 9.0MG

MAKES 4 SERVINGS   **PREPARATION TIME: 45 MINUTES**

½ cup chopped string beans

¼ cup diced bell peppers

¼ cup peeled and diced cucumber

¼ cup thinly sliced Belgian endive leaves

¼ cup diced avocado

¼ cup diced tomato

½ cup diced Seared Asian Tofu (page 184)

2 cups thinly sliced romaine lettuce

1 tablespoon extra-virgin olive oil

2 tablespoons rice wine vinegar

Sea salt and freshly ground black pepper

1. Bring a small pot of water to a boil. Add the string beans and cook for 1 minute to blanch. Rinse under cold water and set aside.

2. In a mixing bowl, combine all the ingredients, including the string beans, and season to taste with salt and pepper. Toss well and serve on chilled plates.

> Use salt and freshly ground pepper to season greens to bring out their fullest flavor.

SALads

✳ ARUGULA WITH CREAMY SHALLOT VINAIGRETTE

CALORIES: 58.5

FAT: 4.4G

PROTEIN: 2.2G

CARBOHYDRATE: 3.5G

CHOLESTEROL: 0MG

SODIUM: 42MG

Mustard and shallots have always been a favorite combination of mine. This is a zippy dressing where a little bit goes a long way. Try sprinkling Lightlife Fakin Bacon Bits on top of this salad for a crunchy meatlike flavor. Chopped grilled chicken or cold poached baby shrimp also go wonderfully in this salad. This dressing will last in your refrigerator for up to 2 weeks in an airtight container.

MAKES 4 SERVINGS	PREPARATION TIME: 30 MINUTES

1 tablespoon egg whites (from about 1 egg)

1 teaspoon whole grain mustard

1 teaspoon Dijon mustard

2 teaspoons minced shallots

1 tablespoon red wine vinegar

¼ cup soft tofu

1 tablespoon walnut oil, or olive or canola oil

Sea salt and freshly ground black pepper

1 bunch arugula leaves, cleaned and dried

8 cherry tomatoes, halved

¼ cup chopped Bermuda onion

1. In a food processor, combine the egg whites, both mustards, shallots, vinegar and tofu. Pulse on/off and slowly drizzle in the oil. Season with salt and pepper to taste.

2. In a mixing bowl, combine the arugula, tomatoes, onion and 2 tablespoons of the vinaigrette. Toss thoroughly, adjust seasoning and serve on chilled plates.

NOTE: There will be enough vinaigrette left to prepare 4 additional salads.

Totally dairy-free Cooking

Pasta and pizza are often overloaded with dairy. Most restaurants will glaze their pasta with a little butter to give it a richer flavor and shiny look just before serving it. Oftentimes, Parmesan cheese is added to a sauce or on top of a pasta as a garnish whether you want it or not. Ravioli and gnocchi are two pasta dishes that are hard to come by without some type of cheese. So how is it possible that I can offer those same dishes in a dairy-free cookbook? Simple! I've cheated the flavors and textures of that added dairy through years of experimenting and perfecting these dairy-free versions of your favorites. In a blind taste test, none of my friends could tell that there was absolutely no dairy in any of these pastas or pizzas. I wish I had bet them money because I could have been a very rich man for every time someone has said "I can't believe there isn't any dairy in this!" See if your family and friends can tell the difference.

For most of the recipes I've suggested the type of pasta to use, but feel free to use any pasta you prefer with any of these sauces. Experiment with different nontraditional pastas like those made with corn, quinoa, rice, spelt or Jerusalem artichoke flour. The key to a great flavor in most pastas is to finish the slightly undercooked pasta in a sauté pan with the sauce. The flavor of the sauce is absorbed into the pasta creating intense flavor without an abundance of sauce. You should be able to taste the pasta *and* the sauce in all of these recipes.

✳ ANGEL HAIR WITH CALIFORNIA PLUM TOMATO, BASIL AND GARLIC SAUCE

CALORIES: 340

FAT: 5.9G

PROTEIN: 10.6G

CARBOHYDRATES: 60.7G

CHOLESTEROL: 0MG

SODIUM: 412MG

This dairy-free pasta is pretty close to my grandma's original recipe. Being a native Californian of Italian heritage, she made the unorthodox move of using California plum tomatoes instead of the traditional Italian tomatoes. The plum tomatoes have less acid in them so she was able to cook them for less time. But if you still swear by Italian tomatoes, note that they might need to be cooked a little bit longer. Sprinkle with soy Parmesan cheese and additional red pepper flakes if desired as a finishing touch. Garnish with whole basil leaves. Try serving this dish with Zesty Turkey Meatballs (page 132) or Millet and Wild Mushroom "Meat" Balls (page 116).

MAKES 8 SERVINGS	PREPARATION TIME: 30 MINUTES

Put a little salt and oil in your rapidly boiling water to keep your pasta from clumping.

1 tablespoon plus 1 teaspoon sea salt

2 tablespoons olive oil

5 cloves garlic, sliced

¼ cup chopped onions

12 basil leaves, chopped

1½ tablespoons tomato paste

One 28-ounce can whole plum tomatoes

½ teaspoon red pepper flakes

1 pound angel hair pasta

1. In a medium stockpot, bring 4 to 6 quarts of water plus 1 tablespoon of the salt to a boil.

2. Meanwhile, in a large nonstick skillet, heat the olive oil for 30 seconds over medium heat. Add the garlic and onions and cook, stirring, until the onions are translucent, about 3 minutes. Add the basil and tomato paste and cook for 2 to 3 minutes. Drain half of the liquid out of the tomatoes and with your hands, crush the whole tomatoes. Add the crushed tomatoes and remaining liquid in the can to the skillet and bring to a simmer. Reduce the heat and simmer for 5 to 7 minutes. Season with the remaining 1 teaspoon salt and the red pepper flakes.

3. In the pot of boiling water, cook the pasta 3 to 4 minutes until it loses it rigidness but is still raw in the center. Drain the undercooked pasta and add it to the tomato sauce. Gently stir the pasta and sauce over medium heat for 4 to 6 minutes, or until fully cooked.

Totally dairy-free Cooking

✳ PENNE WITH SOY VEGETABLE BOLOGNESE SAUCE

I make this at Josie's every year for the New York City Marathon runners who come in looking for a special power meal before the big day. The textured vegetable protein really gives this pasta the extra fuel the runners need to go the distance. If it works for them, imagine what it can do for you!

CALORIES: 472.9

FAT: 5.6G

PROTEIN: 18.6G

CARBOHYDRATES: 87.4G

CHOLESTEROL: 0MG

SODIUM: 139MG

MAKES 4 SERVINGS   **PREPARATION TIME 20 MINUTES**

¼ cup textured vegetable protein
    (TVP)
1 tablespoon olive oil
1 tablespoon minced garlic
½ cup finely diced yellow onions
1 tablespoon tomato paste
¼ cup chopped fresh basil
¼ teaspoon red pepper flakes

½ teaspoon dried oregano
One 28-ounce can whole plum
    tomatoes, drained and chopped
Sea salt
4 cups penne pasta, cooked
    according to package directions
Soy Parmesan cheese, for serving

1. In a small pot, bring ½ cup water to a boil and add the textured vegetable protein. Mix together with a fork and set aside.

2. Heat the olive oil in medium nonstick skillet over medium heat, add the garlic and onions and cook, stirring, until the onions are translucent, about 3 minutes. Add the tomato paste, basil, pepper flakes and oregano and stir. Stir in the tomatoes, bring to a simmer, reduce the heat to low and simmer 5 minutes. Add the TVP and salt, and simmer an additional 5 minutes.

3. Add the cooked pasta to the sauce and mix thoroughly. Serve topped with Parmesan.

Pasta
and
Pizza

✳ 75

✳ LINGUINE WITH TUNA BOLOGNESE SAUCE

CALORIES: 412.8

FAT: 5.1G

PROTEIN: 29G

CARBOHYDRATE: 52.8G

CHOLESTEROL: 38MG

SODIUM: 262MG

This recipe has all of the flavor of a regular meat bolognese. I always think of this dish when I plan a big family dinner. I sometimes use ground chicken in place of the tuna. If you're feeling a bit adventurous, black olives and capers can be added for a Provençal-style flavor.

MAKES 4 SERVINGS   **PREPARATION TIME: 30 MINUTES**

1 tablespoon sea salt, plus additional
    for seasoning

2 tablespoons olive oil

1 tablespoon minced garlic

½ cup minced onions

½ cup finely chopped celery

½ cup finely chopped carrots

2 tablespoons tomato paste

1 teaspoon finely chopped fresh
    thyme

1 teaspoon finely chopped fresh
    oregano

12 ounces yellowfin tuna, finely
    chopped

1 cup red wine, such as Italian red
    table wine

½ teaspoon red pepper flakes

One 28-ounce can whole plum
    tomatoes, drained and lightly
    crushed

Freshly ground black pepper

¼ cup finely chopped fresh parsley

8 ounces linguine

Parsley leaves, for garnish

1. In a medium stockpot, bring to a boil 4 quarts of water with 1 tablespoon of the salt and 1 tablespoon of the olive oil.

2. Meanwhile, heat the remaining 1 tablespoon olive oil in medium skillet over medium heat. Add the garlic and cook until golden, about 1½ minutes. Add the onions, celery and carrots and cook, stirring, for 10 minutes. Add the tomato taste, thyme and oregano and stir well to coat the vegetables. Add the tuna, wine and pepper flakes. Bring to a simmer, reduce the heat to low, and simmer until wine is reduced by half, 5 to 7 minutes. Add the tomatoes and continue to simmer for 10 minutes. Add salt and pepper to taste and add the chopped parsley.

3. Add the linguine to the boiling water and cook until al dente, about 7 minutes. Drain the linguine and add to the sauce. Mix for 2 to 3 minutes until the pasta is well coated. Serve in bowls, garnished with parsley leaves.

Totally dairy-free cooking

✳ SPIRALS WITH TOMATO CHIPOTLE "CREAM" SAUCE

This sauce is so rich in flavor, you'll swear there is cream in it. "Chipotle peppers in adobo" are smoky jalapeño peppers in a tomato sauce and there is no substitute for its flavor. It is available in small cans in most food markets. Keep any leftover peppers in a small plastic container. They will keep in the refrigerator for three weeks. Try serving them with the Zesty Turkey Meatballs (page 132) and pasta.

CALORIES: 282	
FAT: 4.5G	
PROTEIN: 10G	
CARBOHYDRATE: 51.5G	
CHOLESTEROL: 0MG	
SODIUM: 24MG	

MAKES 6 SERVINGS   **PREPARATION TIME: 30 MINUTES**

2 teaspoons sea salt, plus additional for seasoning

2 tablespoons olive oil

2 cloves garlic, thinly sliced

¼ cup chopped onions

¼ cup julienned fresh basil

1 tablespoon finely chopped fresh cilantro

One 28-ounce can whole plum tomatoes, drained and lightly crushed

2 teaspoons chopped chipotle peppers in adobo sauce

1 cup diced canned tomatoes (14½-ounce can) or fresh peeled and diced tomatoes

1 cup plain soy milk

12 ounces spiral-shaped pasta

Cilantro leaves, for garnish

1. In a medium stockpot, bring to a boil 5 quarts of water with 2 teaspoons of the salt and 1 tablespoon of the olive oil.

2. Meanwhile, heat the remaining 1 tablespoon olive oil in a medium nonstick skillet over medium heat. Add the garlic and onion and cook, stirring, until the onions are translucent, about 3 minutes. Toss in the basil, cilantro and plum tomatoes. Cook, stirring, for 3 to 4 minutes. Add the chipotle peppers (be careful not to put too many peppers in—you can always add more but you can't take any out) and diced tomatoes. Cook an additional 3 minutes. Add salt to taste.

3. Transfer the contents of the skillet to a food processor and puree with the soy milk.

4. Add the pasta to the boiling water and cook until al dente 7 to 8 minutes. Drain, and toss the pasta with the sauce. Serve in bowls and garnish with fresh cilantro leaves.

Pasta and Pizza

✳ 77

✳ ZITI WITH VODKA TOMATO SOY "CREAM" SAUCE

CALORIES: 277

FAT: 3.6G

PROTEIN: 8.6G

CARBOHYDRATE: 44.2G

CHOLESTEROL: 0MG

SODIUM: 8MG

Sauté your favorite vegetables, sun-dried tomatoes, shrimp, lobster and/or breast of chicken and add to the sauce when combining with the pasta. This dairy-free "cream" sauce is also great on your favorite tofu-filled ravioli.

MAKES 6 SERVINGS   **PREPARATION TIME: 30 MINUTES**

1 tablespoon sea salt, plus additional
   for seasoning

2 tablespoons olive oil

3 cloves garlic, finely sliced

½ cup chopped onions

5 fresh basil leaves, julienned

¼ teaspoon red pepper flakes

6 tablespoons vodka

One 28-ounce can whole plum
   tomatoes, drained and crushed

1 cup plain soy milk

Freshly ground black pepper

12 ounces ziti

Basil leaves, for garnish

Soy Parmesan cheese, for serving

1. In a medium stockpot, bring to a boil 5 quarts of water with 1 tablespoon of the sea salt and 1 tablespoon of the olive oil.

2. Meanwhile, heat the remaining 1 tablespoon olive oil in a medium nonstick skillet. Add the garlic and onions and cook, stirring, until the onions are translucent, about 3 minutes. Add the basil, pepper flakes and vodka and cook for 2 minutes more. Add the tomatoes, bring to a simmer, reduce the heat to low and simmer for 15 minutes.

3. Transfer the contents of the skillet to a deep storage container and mix with an electric handheld blender (or use a food processor), adding the soy milk slowly. Season with salt and pepper to taste.

4. Add the ziti to the boiling water and cook until al dente 7 to 8 minutes. Drain and toss with the sauce. Serve in bowls with the basil leaves and Parmesan on top.

Totally dairy-free cooking

* BOW TIES WITH SOY PARMESAN, SPINACH, BASIL AND WALNUT PESTO

You can spread this pesto sauce on grilled or toasted bread to create a flavorful bruschetta, or smear it on croutons to zip up any salad. This also mixes well with tomato sauce to give it a unusual pesto flair. For an excellent pasta primavera, sauté your favorite seasonal vegetables and add the pasta to the vegetables. Add a couple of tablespoons of vegetable stock to the dish before mixing in the pesto just before serving.

CALORIES: 329	
FAT: 10G	
PROTEIN: 14G	
CARBOHYDRATE: 48.2G	
CHOLESTEROL: 0MG	
SODIUM: 141MG	

MAKES 4 SERVINGS   **PREPARATION TIME: 30 MINUTES**

1 tablespoon sea salt, plus additional for seasoning

2 tablespoons olive oil

8 ounces bow-tie pasta

¼ cup walnut pieces, lightly toasted in a 350°F oven for 5 minutes

¼ cup tightly packed spinach leaves

½ cup tightly packed basil leaves

Juice of ½ lemon

½ teaspoon minced garlic

2 tablespoons soy Parmesan

2 tablespoons silken tofu

Freshly ground black pepper

Basil leaves, for garnish

> If you want a butter-like sheen and flavor for your cooked pasta, you can drizzle on a little olive oil or soy margarine just before serving.

1. In a medium stockpot, bring to a boil 4 quarts of water, 1 tablespoon of the salt and 1 tablespoon of the olive oil. Add the pasta and cook until al dente, 7 to 8 minutes. Drain.

2. Meanwhile, in a food processor, puree together the remaining 1 tablespoon olive oil plus all the remaining ingredients, except the salt and pepper, until smooth. Add salt and pepper to taste. Add a few tablespoons of water to the food processor if you are having trouble getting the blade to puree at the beginning. Pulse on and off to get the pesto started.

3. In a mixing bowl, toss the hot pasta with the pesto and serve in bowls. Garnish with fresh basil leaves.

Pasta and Pizza

CALORIES: 461.6

FAT: 4.8G

PROTEIN: 41.4G

CARBOHYDRATE: 55.3G

CHOLESTEROL: 81MG

SODIUM: 473MG

Most fettuccine is made with lots of egg yolks so check the ingredients on the package and try to get one that doesn't use yolks—otherwise it will be heavy in fat. This is a light, high-protein version of the traditional recipe. Try substituting De Boles rice fettuccine for regular fettuccine to make an incredible wheat-free meal.

MAKES 4 SERVINGS   **PREPARATION TIME: 25 MINUTES**

1 tablespoon sea salt, plus additional for seasoning

2 teaspoons olive oil

2 teaspoons minced shallots

2 boneless, skinless chicken breasts, pounded thin (5 to 6 ounces total)

¾ cup marsala wine

1 cup thinly sliced shiitake mushrooms

¾ cup Roasted Chicken Stock (page 40)

1 teaspoon balsamic vinegar

8 ounces fettuccine

2 tablespoons finely chopped fresh parsley

6 basil leaves, julienned

Freshly ground black pepper

1. In a medium stockpot, bring 4 to 6 quarts of water with 1 tablespoon of the salt to a boil.

2. Meanwhile, heat the olive oil in a medium nonstick skillet over medium heat. Add the shallots and cook, stirring, until golden, 1 to 2 minutes. Add the chicken and cook until browned on one side, 2 to 3 minutes. Turn over the breasts, add the wine and vinegar and cook until the wine is reduced by half, 3 to 4 minutes.

3. Add the mushrooms and chicken stock to the skillet and continue to cook, 5 to 6 minutes.

4. Add the fettuccine to the boiling water and cook until it loses its rigidness but is still raw in the center, 7 to 8 minutes. Drain the pasta and add to the pan with the chicken. Add the parsley and basil and let the sauce absorb into the underdone pasta for about 2 minutes. Add salt and pepper to taste.

5. Remove the chicken from the pan and set aside. Season the pasta and divide on 4 plates. Slice the chicken breasts and serve over the pasta.

✳ QUICK PIZZA SAUCE

What's better than a slice of good old-fashioned pizza? How about a pizza cooked at home with absolutely no dairy! Lots of pizza places are catching on to the no-cheese pizza idea, but to make a truly tasty pizza it takes a really fabulous sauce. Granular red bell pepper flakes give the sauce a naturally sweet flavor. They are sold in the spice section of health food stores or gourmet supermarkets. I like the Spice Garden brand because it is nonirradiated. As a substitute, you can use 2 teaspoons of finely-diced sweet bell peppers and sauté them with the garlic at the beginning of the recipe.

Use this sauce to produce a piping-hot delicious pizza the whole family will love in 30 minutes or less. Take that pizza place off your speed dial for good!

PER ¼ CUP
CALORIES: 80.4
FAT: 3.1G
PROTEIN: 2.5G
CARBOHYDRATE: 13.4G
CHOLESTEROL: 0MG
SODIUM: 43MG

MAKES 1 CUP, ENOUGH FOR FOUR 8-INCH PIZZAS   **PREPARATION TIME: 15 MINUTES**

2 teaspoons olive oil

1 teaspoon minced garlic

½ cup minced onions

5 basil leaves, julienned

¼ teaspoon red pepper flakes

½ teaspoon dried oregano

2 teaspoons tomato paste

One 14½-ounce can whole plum
    tomatoes, drained and lightly
    crushed

1 teaspoon sweet red bell pepper
    granules, nonirradiated

Sea salt

In a small saucepan over medium heat, heat the olive oil. Add the garlic and onions and cook, stirring, until the onions are translucent, about 3 minutes. Add the basil, pepper flakes, oregano and tomato paste, and cook, stirring, for 2 minutes. Add the tomatoes and bell pepper granules, and simmer for 5 minutes. Season with salt.

Pasta
and
Pizza

✳ SPELT-OAT PIZZA DOUGH

PER 8-INCH PIZZA
CALORIES: 361
FAT: 6.4G
PROTEIN: 27G
CARBOHYDRATE: 69.2G
CHOLESTEROL: 0MG
SODIUM: 473MG

If you're trying dairy-free pizza, why not give wheat-free a try, too? You'll be surprised how much better this dough tastes than traditional pizza dough, and it's better for you. This dough is easy to work with and is a good choice for your first homemade pizza.

MAKES FOUR 8-INCH PIZZA DOUGHS	PREPARATION TIME: 45 MINUTES

2 cups Arrowhead Mills spelt flour

1¼ cups Arrowhead Mills oat flour

1 teaspoon sea salt

1 tablespoon honey

1 tablespoon extra-virgin olive oil

1 tablespoon soft tofu

2¼ teaspoons active dry yeast

1. Measure both flours into a food processor. In a mixing bowl, combine the salt, honey, olive oil, tofu and ¼ cup cool water, and mix well.

2. In a small mixing bowl, dissolve the yeast into ¼ cup warm water (100° to 120°F). Cover and let sit for 10 minutes.

3. Turn the food processor on and slowly drizzle in the honey-tofu mixture. Drizzle in the yeast mixture while it continues to run. The dough should form around the blade at this time. Put the dough on a lightly floured surface and knead the dough for several minutes until smooth. Sprinkle a little extra flour into the dough if it becomes sticky as you are kneading. Transfer the dough into a covered container and let rest at 70° to 80°F for 30 minutes.

4. Cut the dough into 4 even pieces and form into tight dough balls. At this point you can roll out the pizza dough or refrigerate the balls until you are ready to make the pizza. Note: Allow 1 hour for the refrigerated pizza dough to sit at room temperature before rolling it out.

5. With a rolling pin, gently roll out the dough balls going from the center out, forming a round flat disk. Ideally you would like an 8-inch diameter that is a bit thicker around the edges. With a little bit of practice you can do this with your hands, eliminating the rolling pin altogether.

Totally
dairy-free
Cooking

✳ CORN, SPELT AND SOY PIZZA DOUGH

This pizza dough can be used for any of the pizza recipes in this book. It has a slightly crisper texture than the Spelt-Oat Pizza Dough (page 82) when cooked but is a bit harder to work with, so master that one before tackling this more delicate recipe.

MAKES FOUR 8-INCH PIZZA DOUGHS	PREPARATION TIME: 45 MINUTES

1¼ cups corn flour

½ cup soy flour

1½ cups Arrowhead Mills spelt flour

1 teaspoon sea salt

1 tablespoon honey

1 tablespoon extra-virgin olive oil

1 tablespoon soft tofu

2¼ teaspoons active dry yeast

1. In a food processor, mix all of the flours. In a mixing bowl, combine the salt, honey, olive oil, tofu and ¼ cup of cool water. Mix well.

2. In a small mixing bowl, dissolve the yeast into ¼ cup of warm water (100° to 120°F). Cover and let sit for 10 minutes.

3. Turn the food processor on and slowly drizzle in the honey-tofu mixture. Drizzle in the yeast mixture while it continues to run. The dough should form around the blade at this time. Put the dough on a lightly floured surface and knead for several minutes until smooth. Sprinkle a little extra flour into the dough if it becomes sticky as you are kneading. Transfer the dough into a covered container and let rest at 70° to 80° F for 30 minutes.

4. Cut the dough into 4 even pieces and form into tight dough balls. At this point you can roll out the pizza dough or refrigerate the balls until you are ready to make pizza. Note: Allow 1 hour for refrigerated pizza dough to sit at room temperature before rolling it out.

5. With a rolling pin, gently roll out the dough balls going from the center out, forming a round flat disk. Ideally you would like an 8-inch diameter that is a bit thicker around the edges. With a little bit of practice you can do this with your hands, eliminating the rolling pin altogether.

Pasta
and
Pizza

✳ PIZZA MARGHERITA

A pizza stone will bring your pizza making skills to a whole new level. The stone helps the crust achieve the crispness that you are familiar with from your local pizza shop.

If you are a connoisseur of pizza and especially thin crusted ones, investing in an inexpensive pizza–baking stone will greatly improve the texture and flavor of your crust. Always preheat your oven to 500°F for 30 minutes before putting the pie in the oven. A pizza usually takes around 6 to 8 minutes of baking time if the oven is completely preheated. The stone slightly speeds up the cooking process.

MAKES ONE 8-INCH PIZZA　　　　　　　　**PREPARATION TIME: 12 MINUTES**

3 to 4 tablespoons Quick Pizza Sauce (page 81)

1 recipe Spelt-Oat Pizza Dough (page 82)

1 tablespoon soy Parmesan

6 basil leaves, julienned

2 ounces soy mozzarella cheese, grated (approximately ½ cup)

1. Preheat the oven to 500°F. Spread the pizza sauce over the rolled out dough. Sprinkle the Parmesan then the basil over the sauce. Spread the mozzarella over the dough.

2. Bake the pizza on a pizza stone or on a nonstick baking tray or cookie sheet for 6 to 7 minutes.

NOTE: For all pizzas, when using a stone, sprinkle a little bit of coarse cornmeal on the hot stone before putting the pizza dough on it to prevent sticking.

Totally dairy-free cooking

✴ PIZZA PESTO WITH CHICKEN SAUSAGE

This is a dairy-free designer pizza. You can substitute soy vegetarian sausage for the chicken sausage for a meat-free alternative. The flavor is surprisingly full and pleasing.

MAKES ONE 8-INCH PIZZA　　　　　　　**PREPARATION TIME: 15 MINUTES**

4 ounces fully-cooked chicken
   sausage links, sliced thin

1 tablespoon Miso Basil Lime Pesto
   (page 147) or any other pesto in
   this book

1 recipe Spelt-Oat Pizza Dough
   (page 82)

2 to 3 tablespoons Quick Pizza Sauce
   (page 81)

2 ounces soy mozzarella cheese
   (approximately ½ cup grated)

PER 8-INCH PIZZA
CALORIES: 415.6
FAT: 9.8G
PROTEIN: 19.9G
CARBOHYDRATE: 75.1G
CHOLESTEROL: 0MG
SODIUM: 504MG

1. Preheat the oven to 500°F for 30 minutes. In a nonstick skillet over medium heat, quickly cook the sausage, stirring, for 2 to 3 minutes. Set aside.

2. Spread the pesto over the lightly rolled out dough, then spread the sauce. Sprinkle the mozzarella over the dough. Spread the sausage around the pizza. Bake on a pizza stone or on a nonstick baking tray or cookie sheet for 6 to 7 minutes.

Pasta
and
Pizza

PER 8-INCH PIZZA

CALORIES: 438

FAT: 10.5G

PROTEIN: 23G

CARBOHYDRATE: 77G

CHOLESTEROL: 0MG

SODIUM: 597MG

This is a great pizza with a unique smoky taste from the soy bacon bits, sure to please kids and adults.

MAKES ONE 8-INCH PIZZA **PREPARATION TIME: 15 MINUTES**

3 to 4 tablespoons Quick Pizza Sauce
   (page 81)
1 recipe Spelt-Oat Pizza Dough
   (page 82)
2 teaspoons Lightlife Fakin Bacon Bits

2 teaspoons soy Parmesan
6 basil leaves, julienned
2 ounces soy mozzarella cheese,
   grated (approximately ½ cup)

1. Preheat the oven to 500°F for 30 minutes. Spread the sauce over the dough. Sprinkle the bacon bits onto the sauce. Then sprinkle the soy Parmesan and the basil around the dough. Finally, spread the mozzarella over the whole pie.

2. Bake on a pizza stone or on a nonstick baking tray or cookie sheet for 6 to 7 minutes.

Totally
dairy-free
cooking

✳Lobster, Corn and Jalapeño Soy Jack Quesadilla (page 36) with Three-Pepper Salsa (page 170)

✳ New England–Style Clam Chowder (page 48)

✳ Sesame Seared Tuna with Miso Tofu Vinaigrette (page 96) and Mango-Scallion Sticky Rice (page 188)

✳ Herb Broiled Shrimp (page 93) with Steamed Broccoli in Basil, White Wine and Garlic Broth (page 185)

✳ Ziti with Vodka Tomato Soy "Cream" Sauce (page 78) and Pizza with Soy Bacon, Tomato and Basil (page 86)

✳ Spinach Salad with Roasted Beets and Seared Asian Tofu (page 67)

✳ Baked Corn Macaroni with Soy Jalapeño Jack and Vegetables (page 106) and Roasted Portobello and Soy Mozzarella Melt (page 109)

✳ Three-Grain Super Pancakes (page 202) served with fresh berries (*opposite*)

✳ Soy Creamed Spinach (page 178) and Three-Potato Mash (page 180)

✳ Chocolate Chip Spelt Cookies (page 214), Corn and Sun-Dried Cranberry Biscotti (page 211), Almond Biscotti (page 210) with Frozen Soy-Banana Cappuccino (page 232)

Fish is a healthful alternative meal. It's easy to prepare and offers a plethora of variations. I like to eat a lot of protein and I find that fish gives me the opportunity to experiment with different sauces on a myriad of textures. If you like a particular sauce used in a recipe, try it on several different kinds of fish. I've given suggestions in almost every recipe. For instance, if you don't like swordfish, you can replace it with tuna, tilapia, snapper or halibut and still maintain the excellent flavors in the Mediterranean Swordfish recipe (page 95). Get used to experimenting with fish, and I'm sure your tastebuds will always be satisfied.

When buying fresh fish, make sure it comes from a reputable fishmonger who does enough volume of business to keep a constant turnover of fresh seafood. Ask when the fish arrived, whether it was frozen or fresh, and if the fishmonger would suggest a particular "catch of the day." Fresh fish should look translucent in color and should not have a strong fishy odor. Don't let fresh fish sit out too long before cooking, and make sure that you use it within forty-eight hours of purchase. Always rinse the fish in cold water before seasoning.

✳ MONKFISH "OSSO BUCO" WITH TOMATO SAFFRON SOY SAUCE

CALORIES: 128.9

FAT: 6G

PROTEIN: 14.6G

CARBOHYDRATE: 4.3G

CHOLESTEROL: 21MG

SODIUM: 61MG

When buying fish for this recipe, make sure your fishmonger leaves the center vertebrae bone in the fish. The flavor is so rich and robust, you'll swear it contains cream. Be careful when using the saffron for seasoning. It has a very pungent flavor. You can always add more if you prefer that taste.

MAKES 4 SERVINGS	PREPARATION TIME: 1 HOUR

4 ripe plum tomatoes
Sea salt and freshly ground black
   pepper
1 head garlic
½ teaspoon olive oil
Four 8-ounce monkfish steaks, with
   center bone (vertabrae)

1 cup plain soy milk
1 pinch saffron threads
1 tablespoon soy margarine
1 teaspoon minced fresh chives, or
   ½ teaspoon dried

When buying fish, ideally, you want to buy it whole. Whole fish stays fresh longer because it is still in its natural preservative, its own skin. It will last twice as long in your refrigerator than a filleted one. If you want the fish filleted, ask your fishmonger to do it right in front of you, so you know it's fresh.

1. Preheat the oven to 275°F. Cut the tomatoes in half lengthwise and season with salt and pepper. Cut the top off of the garlic head and drizzle olive oil over it. Place in a baking tray with the tomatoes and roast for 1 hour. When finished, increase the oven temperature to 350°F.

2. Fifteen minutes before the tomatoes finish roasting, season the monkfish steaks with salt and pepper. Spray a nonstick skillet with canola oil spray and set over medium heat. Add the monkfish and sear all 4 sides, about 2 minutes per side. Set aside to rest at room temperature while the tomatoes and garlic are in the oven.

3. Remove the garlic cloves from the head and chop the tomato halves into 4 pieces each. Cook the tomatoes and garlic in a nonstick skillet over medium heat, stirring, for 2 to 3 minutes. Add the soy milk and saffron and mix with a whisk, breaking up the tomatoes in the process. Whisk in the margarine to finish the sauce and season with the chives and salt and pepper to taste. Set the sauce aside and keep warm.

4. Finish cooking the seared monkfish in the oven on a baking tray for 8 to 10 minutes. Serve the monkfish with the sauce on top.

Totally dairy-free cooking

90 ✳

✳ SEARED HALIBUT WITH LEMON CAPER SOY "BEURRE BLANC"

Beurre blanc, a butter-flavored sauce, was very popular in restaurants in the '80s. This soy version will take you into the next millennium with all of the same flavor minus the extra fat and dairy.

PER ¼ CUP SAUCE
CALORIES: 240.4
FAT: 9G
PROTEIN: 23.3G
CARBOHYDRATE: 13.3G
CHOLESTEROL: 33MG
SODIUM: 150MG

MAKES 4 SERVINGS **PREPARATION TIME: 45 MINUTES**

½ cup dry white wine

1 small lemon, peeled and sliced

½ cup chopped onions

1 tablespoons honey

½ cup fresh orange juice (from 1 to 2 oranges)

6 ounces plain soy milk

2 tablespoons soy margarine

Sea salt and freshly ground black pepper

1 tablespoon capers, rinsed and drained

1 teaspoon thinly sliced fresh chives

Four 6-ounce halibut fillets

1. In a small saucepan, bring the wine, sliced lemon, onions, honey and orange juice to a boil. Reduce the heat and simmer until the liquid is reduced to a syrup, 12 to 15 minutes. (Be careful not to reduce too fast and burn the reduction.) Add the soy milk and remove from the heat. Whisk in the margarine and season with salt and pepper to taste. Strain through a fine-mesh strainer and mix in the capers and chives. Set aside in a warm place.

2. Preheat the oven to 350°F. Season the halibut on both sides with salt and pepper. Spray a nonstick skillet with canola oil spray and sear the fish on both sides over medium heat until lightly browned, 2 to 3 minutes per side. Finish cooking the fillets in the oven on a baking tray for an additional 5 to 7 minutes.

3. Place the cooked fillets on serving plates and spoon ¼ of the sauce over each piece.

Fish and Seafood

✳ GARLIC-HERB-CRUSTED TILAPIA

CALORIES: 127.4

FAT: 1.6G

PROTEIN: 19.2G

CARBOHYDRATE: 10.6G

CHOLESTEROL: 31MG

SODIUM: 322MG

Tilapia is the nonseafood lovers' fish. It has a very neutral flavor. The oven-dried crust is also terrific on chicken, snapper, grouper or sea bass. Make a little extra and keep it in a sealed container in the refrigerator until you want to use it.

MAKES 4 SERVINGS	PREPARATION TIME: 1¼ HOURS

¼ cup thinly sliced garlic

½ teaspoon sea salt

2 tablespoons whole wheat bread crumbs

1 teaspoon minced fresh tarragon

1 teaspoon minced fresh oregano, or ½ teaspoon dried

1 teaspoon minced fresh thyme, or ½ teaspoon dried

1 teaspoon minced fresh chervil

Four 6-ounce tilapia or red snapper fillets

2 lemons

1. Preheat the oven to 275°F. Toss the garlic with the salt and place on a nonstick baking tray. Roast for 30 to 35 minutes until dry.

2. In a small food processor, puree the garlic with the bread crumbs and herbs. Keep in a sealed container in a cool area until ready to use.

3. Lightly dredge both sides of the fish fillets with the garlic-herb puree.

4. Spray a nonstick skillet with canola oil spray. Cook the fish over medium-low heat, 3 to 4 minutes on each side. Check the center of each fillet to see if it is cooked through. If the fillets are thick, they can be finished in a 350°F oven for several minutes. Serve with ½ lemon on each plate.

Totally dairy-free Cooking

✳ HERB BROILED SHRIMP

This was one of my grandmother Josephina's favorite recipes. Her version was *full* of dairy, but mine isn't! (Sorry, Grandma . . .) Sourdough bread crumbs are excellent when available or if you have the time to make them. This dish is great with Tomato and Soy Mozzarella Polenta (page 179) and steamed asparagus or the Steamed Broccoli in Basil, White Wine and Garlic Broth (page 185). The sauce is also great on broiled scallops or lobster.

CALORIES: 227.1	
FAT: 12.6G	
PROTEIN: 20G	
CARBOHYDRATE: 5.8G	
CHOLESTEROL: 175MG	
SODIUM: 533MG	

MAKES 8 SERVINGS　　　　　　　　**PREPARATION TIME: 30 MINUTES**

2 pounds large shrimp (16 to 20 per pound size)

4 ounces soy margarine

1 teaspoon minced fresh cilantro

1 teaspoon minced fresh tarragon

1 teaspoon minced fresh basil

1 clove garlic, minced

1 teaspoon fresh lemon juice

1 teaspoon brandy, or cooking sherry

Sea salt and freshly ground black pepper

½ cup whole wheat bread crumbs

½ teaspoon Old Bay Seasoning

6 tablespoons white wine

1. Clean and devein the shrimp, leaving the tail intact. To butterfly the shrimp, split them three quarters of the way through by following the vein line with a paring knife.

2. In a mixing bowl, combine the margarine with the cilantro, tarragon, basil, garlic, lemon juice and brandy. Season with salt and pepper. In another bowl, mix the bread crumbs with the Old Bay.

3. Preheat the broiler. Rub approximately ¾ teaspoon of the margarine mixture on each butterflied shrimp. Sprinkle the bread crumbs over the shrimp and place on a nonstick baking sheet (with an edge).

4. Broil the shrimp for 3 minutes. Remove from the broiler, drizzle the wine over the shrimp. Set the oven to 400°F and bake the shrimp in the oven for 3 more minutes or until cooked through.

Fish and Seafood

✳ 93

✳ HUMMUS-CRUSTED SALMON WITH CUCUMBER AND TOMATO SALSA

CALORIES: 267.4

FAT: 9.7G

PROTEIN: 35.5G

CARBOHYDRATE: 7.6G

CHOLESTEROL: 89MG

SODIUM: 175MG

This Mediterranean twist on salmon is high in flavor and easy to make. The hummus crust gives a unique taste to salmon and can also be used when making halibut or sea bass. This dish goes well with the Root Vegetable Puree (page 183) and your favorite steamed seasonal green leafy vegetable. Add ½ cup of diced fresh mango to the salsa for a tropical addition to this Middle Eastern dish.

MAKES 4 SERVINGS	PREPARATION TIME: 45 MINUTES

1 ripe beefsteak tomato

¾ cup peeled, seeded and diced
   cucumbers

1 tablespoon diced Bermuda onion

2 teaspoons olive oil

1 tablespoon rice wine vinegar

1½ teaspoons rice wine (*mirin*)

1½ teaspoons chopped fresh dill

Sea salt and freshly ground black pepper

Four 6-ounce salmon fillets, skin
   removed

¼ cup Black Bean Hummus (page
   160), substituting white beans

4 teaspoons whole wheat bread
   crumbs

Lemon wedges, for serving

1. In a small stockpot, bring 2 quarts of water to a boil. Make an X-shaped shallow incision with a paring knife on the bottom of the tomato, to make peeling easier. Add to the boiling water and blanch for 1 minute. Rinse the tomato under cold water to remove the skin and cut into medium dice.

2. In a mixing bowl, combine the cucumbers, tomato, and onions. Add the olive oil, vinegar, wine and dill. Season with salt and pepper and toss gently. Set aside or refrigerate if making ahead.

3. Preheat the broiler. Spray a nonstick skillet with canola oil spray and set over medium heat. Season the salmon fillets with salt and pepper. Sear the salmon for 3 to 4 minutes on each side.

4. Place the salmon on a nonstick baking tray and spread about 1 tablespoon of hummus evenly over each fillet. Sprinkle 1 teaspoon of bread crumbs on each over the hummus. Finish the salmon under the broiler for 3 to 4 minutes to get a golden brown crust.

5. Serve with cucumber–tomato salsa spooned over the top and lemon wedges on the side.

Totally
dairy-free
cooking

✳ MEDITERRANEAN SWORDFISH

This is a quick and easy recipe that will delight even the most discriminating palate. I love Greek olives, and they add an extra zest to any fish. If you don't like swordfish, you can substitute tuna, tilapia, snapper or halibut.

CALORIES: 289

FAT: 11.3G

PROTEIN: 35.7G

CARBOHYDRATE: 11.5G

CHOLESTEROL: 66MG

SODIUM: 448MG

MAKES 4 SERVINGS   **PREPARATION TIME: 30 MINUTES**

Four 6- to 7-ounce swordfish steaks
Sea salt and freshly ground black
   pepper
2 teaspoons olive oil
1½ teaspoons minced garlic
¼ cup balsamic vinegar
1½ teaspoons minced fresh oregano,
   or ½ teaspoon dried

1 tablespoon minced fresh parsley
½ cup halved Greek olives
½ cup julienned sun-dried tomatoes
   (dry, not the oil-packed variety)
1½ cups halved cherry tomatoes
½ bunch arugula, cleaned well

1. Season the swordfish steaks with salt and pepper. Grill the swordfish on an outdoor grill for 3 to 4 minutes on each side or use a nonstick grill pan on the stove top.

2. In a medium nonstick skillet, heat the olive oil over medium heat. Add the garlic and cook, stirring, until golden, about 1 minute. Add the vinegar and ¼ cup of water, then add the oregano, parsley, olives, sun-dried tomatoes, and cherry tomatoes. Cook, stirring, for 3 to 5 minutes.

3. Arrange the arugula in the center of 4 serving plates. Place a piece of swordfish on each plate. Spoon ½ cup sauce over each piece of swordfish.

> When buying fish, press it with your finger. The fish should be firm and elastic and your finger should not leave an indentation. The eyes should be clear and full, not milky and sunken, and the gills should be bright red, not an ashen gray.

Fish
and
Seafood

✳ 95

✳ SESAME SEARED TUNA WITH MISO TOFU VINAIGRETTE

CALORIES: 301.4

FAT: 10.8G

PROTEIN: 42.7G

CARBOHYDRATE: 6.3G

CHOLESTEROL: 65MG

SODIUM: 479MG

The versatile miso tofu vinaigrette tastes great spooned over this seared tuna or try it over chicken and vegetables right off the grill. For a spicier version, coat the fillet or steak with ground coriander, black pepper and salt. Try slicing thick pieces of cooked fish steak and arrange them around the sauce for a fancier presentation.

MAKES 4 SERVINGS	PREPARATION TIME: 15 MINUTES

1 tablespoon barley miso or regular miso

1 tablespoon tamari soy sauce

1 tablespoon rice wine (mirin)

1 tablespoon rice wine vinegar

½ cup water

Juice of ½ lime

2 ounces soft tofu

2 scallions, trimmed and thinly sliced

Four 6-ounce tuna steaks, about 1 inch thick

Sea salt and freshly ground black pepper

4 teaspoons black sesame seeds

Mango-Scallion Sticky Rice (page 188) for serving

1. Mix together the miso, soy sauce, rice wine, vinegar, water, lime juice and tofu with an electric hand mixer or food processor. Mix in the sliced scallions by hand and set the sauce aside.

2. Season the tuna steaks with sea salt and ground black pepper. Coat one side of the steak with sesame seeds. Coat a nonstick skillet with canola oil spray and set over medium heat for at least 1 minute to heat the pan. Add the tuna to the pan, sesame seed side first, to sear for 2 to 3 minutes. Turn over the fish and finish cooking to the desired doneness, 2 to 3 minutes more for medium. Remove from the heat.

3. Spoon the sauce among four serving plates. Slice each tuna steak in half and place two halves on top of the sauce on each serving plate. Serve with Mango-Scallion Sticky Rice.

Totally dairy-free cooking

CHILEAN SEA BASS WITH CHIPOTLE ORANGE GLAZE

Chilean sea bass is an extremely popular, thick succulent white fish that comes fresh or frozen. It thaws out very nicely and it's hard to distinguish fresh from frozen. This is a fast, lowfat, high protein and incredible tasting dish full of clean exotic flavors. It goes well with the Roasted Taro Root (page 192); be sure to start the taro root in the oven first so everything will be ready at the same time.

CALORIES: 213.4

FAT: 3.6G

PROTEIN: 32.1G

CARBOHYDRATE: 12G

CHOLESTEROL: 70MG

SODIUM: 117MG

MAKES 4 SERVINGS   **PREPARATION TIME: 30 MINUTES**

1¼ cups fresh orange juice (from about 4 oranges)

Juice of 1 lime

1 teaspoon minced fresh ginger

1 teaspoon minced canned chipotle pepper

1 teaspoon arrowroot

1 teaspoon honey

Four 6-ounce Chilean sea bass fillets (1½ pounds)

Sea salt and freshly ground black pepper

1. In a small saucepan, bring the orange juice, lime juice, ginger, and chipotle pepper to a boil. Reduce the heat and simmer until reduced by half, 8 to 10 minutes.

2. In a small bowl, mix together the arrowroot with 2 teaspoons of water. Add it to the simmering sauce along with the honey, cook for 2 minutes more, remove from the heat, and set aside in a warm place.

3. Preheat the oven to 350°F. Spray a nonstick skillet with canola oil spray. Season all the sides of the Chilean sea bass with salt and black pepper and sear the bass for 2 minutes on each of the 4 sides over medium heat. Transfer the fillets to a baking tray and spoon a tablespoon of the glaze over each fillet. Roast in the oven for 8 to 10 minutes, or until the fish is medium done. Add additional glaze before serving.

Fish and Seafood

✳ SEARED YELLOWFIN TUNA BURGER

CALORIES: 131.9

FAT: 1.1G

PROTEIN: 26.8G

CARBOHYDRATE: 1.3G

CHOLESTEROL: 51MG

SODIUM: 207MG

We make a limited amount of these at Josie's every night and they are so popular, some of our patrons call up in advance to reserve them. You may very well give up beef burgers for good after tasting these. Try it with my Miso Wasabi Coulis (page 149) or Basic Ketchup (page 165). Serve open-faced on your favorite toasted bread or roll with pickled ginger. In the summer months, try grilling the burgers on a clean, well-oiled grill.

MAKES 4 SERVINGS	PREPARATION TIME: 1 HOUR

1 pound yellowfin tuna, ground or
    finely chopped
1½ teaspoons rice wine (*mirin*)
1½ teaspoons tamari soy sauce

1½ teaspoons *wasabi* powder
¼ teaspoon ground coriander
Freshly ground black pepper to taste

1. In a mixing bowl, thoroughly mix all the ingredients together. Form the mixture into 4 patties. Refrigerate for 30 minutes to set.

2. Set a nonstick skillet over medium heat and spray with canola oil spray. Add the patties to the pan and sear for 3 to 4 minutes on each side. For well-done burgers you may want to finish cooking them on a baking tray in a preheated 350°F oven for 5 to 7 minutes.

NOTES: Caution! Use only the freshest ground tuna from a reputable fishmonger. Once tuna is ground, it is exposed to additional bacteria and therefore should be cooked on the same day as it is ground. If you are grinding it yourself, be sure that all the grinding apparatus is sanitized before and after each use. This will greatly reduce the chances of excessive bacteria.

Totally dairy-free cooking

✳ STIR-FRIED SHRIMP WITH YUCA IN COCONUT-CURRY CREAM

This is a super flavorful and satisfying stir-fry that is low in fat yet still has a creamy flavor. The carrot juice adds richness and sweetness. Try to use fresh carrot juice if you have a juicer. Yuca is a tuberous root vegetable found in the potato section of most full-service supermarkets. It is always readily available in Latin American specialty markets. Try the Mango-Scallion Sticky Rice (page 188) as a side dish.

CALORIES: 200.2

FAT: 3.2G

PROTEIN: 15.9G

CARBOHYDRATE: 31.5G

CHOLESTEROL: 86MG

SODIUM: 104MG

MAKES 4 SERVINGS   **PREPARATION TIME: 1¼ HOURS**

2 tablespoons unsweetened coconut
    milk

2 tablespoons honey

1 tablespoon minced fresh ginger

1 teaspoon curry powder

¼ cup carrot juice

1 teaspoon Bragg's Liquid Amino, or
    tamari soy sauce

Juice of 1 lime

¼ teaspoon ground coriander

Freshly ground black pepper

8 ounces medium shrimp, peeled,
    deveined and tails removed

1 cup peeled and sliced yuca root

1 cup peeled and sliced sweet potato

16 string beans, trimmed

½ cup diced bell peppers

Sea salt

1 tablespoon trimmed and thinly
    sliced scallions

1 tablespoon whole fresh cilantro
    leaves

1. In a mixing bowl, combine the coconut milk, honey, ginger, curry powder, carrot juice, Bragg's Liquid Amino, lime juice, coriander and black pepper to taste and whisk very well. Remove ¼ cup of this marinade and set aside. Add the shrimp to the remaining marinade and refrigerate for a minimum of 45 minutes.

2. Spray a nonstick wok with canola oil spray and heat over medium heat. Add the yuca and sweet potato. Cook, stirring, for 2 to 3 minutes. Add the string beans and bell peppers. Add the ¼ cup reserved marinade and continue to cook, stirring, for 4 to 5 minutes. Season the vegetables with salt and pepper to taste. Drain the shrimp and add to the wok. Cook, stirring, for 2 to 3 minutes. Add the scallions and cilantro and serve.

Fish
and
Seafood

CALORIES: 145.9	
FAT: 3.3G	
PROTEIN: 13.9G	
CARBOHYDRATE: 14.7G	
CHOLESTEROL: 54MG	
SODIUM: 487MG	

This stir-fry is great for entertaining and combines an eclectic mix of ingredients. You can replace the lobster with scallops, shrimp or even use a combination of all three. Keep a little extra water and/or stock nearby to add to the stir-fry instead of oil if it seems too dry in the wok.

MAKES 4 SERVINGS **PREPARATION TIME: 30 MINUTES**

2 teaspoons olive oil

2 cups peeled and sliced butternut squash (about ¾ pound)

2 cups sliced (on bias) asparagus (about ¾ pound)

½ cup julienned red bell peppers

1 cup cooked and sliced lobster meat

½ cup Stir-fry Sauce (page 154)

¼ cup trimmed and thinly sliced scallions

Freshly ground black pepper

Oil-free Tamari Brown Rice (page 187)

1. Heat the olive oil in a nonstick wok over medium heat. Add the squash and cook, stirring, for 3 to 4 minutes. Add the asparagus, bell peppers and 2 tablespoons water and continue to cook, stirring, for 3 to 4 minutes more.

2. Toss in the lobster, Stir-fry Sauce and scallions. Cook an additional 1 minute and serve over the rice.

Totally
dairy-free
cooking

✳ SUPER BOWL TUNA AND THREE-BEAN CHILI

While writing this cookbook, I often had my friends try new recipes as they were created. What better reason to have chili than the Super Bowl? My team may have lost, but my chili was the real winner that day! Even my die-hard meat-and-potato fans were completely satiated. This is best if you let it sit for one to two hours to develop the flavors, and reheat before serving. Serve with diced avocado mixed with a little bit of your favorite salsa and fresh lime juice. You can replace the ground tuna with ground turkey, chicken or beef if desired.

CALORIES: 211.6

FAT: 4.0G

PROTEIN: 18.1G

CARBOHYDRATE: 24.9G

CHOLESTEROL: 20MG

SODIUM: 261MG

MAKES 10 SERVINGS   **PREPARATION TIME: 50 MINUTES**

1 tablespoon olive oil

2 teaspoons minced garlic

1 cup chopped onions

½ cup chopped celery

½ cup chopped carrots

One 28-ounce can plum tomatoes, drained

1 tablespoon minced chipotle pepper, or jalapeño

1 pound fresh yellowfin or albacore tuna, finely chopped or ground

1 teaspoon ground cumin

1 teaspoon chili powder

1 teaspoon ground coriander

1½ teaspoons sea salt

½ teaspoon freshly ground black pepper

1 cup beer, preferably Mexican dark

One 15-ounce can cooked pinto beans, drained and rinsed

One 15-ounce can cooked white beans, drained and rinsed

One 15-ounce can cooked black soy beans (or regular black beans), drained and rinsed

1 tablespoon tomato paste

¼ cup trimmed and finely sliced scallions

¼ cup minced fresh cilantro

2 cups cooked brown rice

To remove the fish smell from your hands, rinse them thoroughly, then rub them with lemon juice or fresh parsley. (This works for garlic, onions and shallots, too.)

1. In a medium heavy-duty saucepan, heat the olive oil over medium heat. Add the garlic and onions and cook, stirring, until the onions are translucent, about 3 minutes. Add the celery and carrots and cook, stirring, for 5 minutes more. Crush the plum tomatoes by hand and add to the pot. Add the chipotle pepper (careful not to add too much if you're sensitive to spices) and simmer for 5 minutes.

Fish and Seafood

2. In a mixing bowl, hand mix the tuna, cumin, chili, coriander, salt and black pepper. Add this mixture to the saucepan and stir. Add the beer, stir and simmer for 5 minutes more. Mix in all 3 beans and the tomato paste and continue to simmer until heated through.

3. Before serving, add the scallions, cilantro and rice.

Totally
daiRy-free
Cooking

A lot of people still think of vegetarian cooking as dull and tasteless, yet their curiosity is often piqued by the numerous vegetarian offerings found in almost every restaurant. I'll let you in on a little secret. Many restaurants load their vegetarian dishes with dairy. And sometimes, chefs will use a chicken stock to give vegetarian meals extra flavor, especially with pastas and grains. When I opened Josie's, I proved that more healthful vegetarian cooking could not only be gourmet but also satisfy even the pickiest palate.

In most cases, the recipes in this chapter are an excellent source of protein, which is something often lacking in meatless meals. Vegetarian dishes are usually very high in carbohydrates and starchy foods, and are often loaded with fat and calories. These delicious offerings are the most popular dishes served at my restaurants, ones that even the choosiest meat eater can enjoy.

CALORIES: 514.6	
FAT: 9.8G	
PROTEIN: 16.6G	
CARBOHYDRATE: 94.7G	
CHOLESTEROL: 0MG	
SODIUM: 287MG	

You still get all of the great cheesy taste of this American classic comfort food but without any of the dairy. Corn macaroni is a unique substitute for the common wheat variety, giving this dish an unusual twist. The jalapeño soy cheese adds a little extra punch.

MAKES 6 SERVINGS   **PREPARATION TIME: 40 MINUTES**

1 teaspoon soy margarine
1 clove garlic, minced
½ cup chopped onions
1 cup sliced zucchini
1 cup sliced mushrooms, such as cremini or shiitake
1¼ cups plain soy milk

1 teaspoon arrowroot
½ cup grated soy jalapeño Jack
3 cups cooked De Boles elbow corn macaroni
2 tablespoons grated soy Parmesan
Sea salt and freshly ground black pepper

1. Preheat the oven to 350°F. In a nonstick skillet over medium heat, melt the margarine. Add the garlic and onions and cook, stirring, until the onions are translucent, about 5 minutes. Add the zucchini and mushrooms and cook, stirring, for 5 minutes. Transfer the vegetable mixture to a mixing bowl.

2. In a nonstick pot, add the soy milk and bring to a simmer. Mix the arrowroot with 2 tablespoons of water and whisk into the milk along with the jalapeño Jack. Add the pasta and mix thoroughly. Add the Parmesan and transfer to the mixing bowl with the cooked vegetables. Season with salt and pepper to taste. Mix together and place in a nonstick loaf pan.

3. Bake uncovered for 20 to 25 minutes. Cut into 6 pieces and serve.

Totally dairy-free cooking

✳ TEMPEH BACON, SOY CHEDDAR, TOMATO AND ONION QUESADILLA

The flavor of the tempeh bacon is so delicious, you'll hardly believe that it isn't really meat. Similar to the Grilled Soy Cheddar Cheese and Fakin Bacon Sandwich on page 188, this vegetarian treat is so gooey, rich and delicious, you won't miss the dairy.

PER WHOLE QUESADILLA

CALORIES: 226.2

FAT: 9.6G

PROTEIN: 11.3G

CARBOHYDRATE: 25.2G

CHOLESTEROL: 0MG

SODIUM: 492MG

MAKES ONE 8-INCH QUESADILLA   **PREPARATION TIME: 15 MINUTES**

Two 8-inch whole grain flour tortillas

2 ounces soy cheddar, grated (½ cup)

1 tablespoon Lightlife Fakin Bacon Bits

¼ cup chopped tomatoes

¼ cup chopped red onions

2 tablespoons Guacamole (page 161) or sliced avocado

1. Place 1 tortilla on a flat surface and distribute the cheddar evenly around the tortilla. Evenly sprinkle the bacon bits, tomatoes and onions over the top.

2. Spray a nonstick skillet with canola oil spray and set over medium heat. Place the open-faced tortilla in the pan. Cook until lightly browned on the bottom, then place the second tortilla over the top, when the cheese begins to melt. Press lightly with your fingers. To flip the quesadilla, slide it out onto a plate. Put another plate over the top and turn it upside down. Slide the quesadilla back into the pan (now upside down), and cook until the cheese is melted inside. Remove the quesadilla from the pan and cut it into 6 to 8 pieces. Serve with a tiny dollop of guacamole or sliced avocado in the center of individual wedges. It tastes equally good with a dollop of salsa.

Vegetarian Dishes

CALORIES: 388.2

FAT: 13.9G

PROTEIN: 24.2G

CARBOHYDRATE: 45.6G

CHOLESTEROL: 0MG

SODIUM: 803MG

These vegetarian enchiladas are quite filling and full of traditional Mexican flavors. This recipe is pretty spicy so if you want to tame it down a bit, replace the chipotle sauce with ¾ cup tomato sauce and heat it with ¼ cup plain soy milk. You'll still have a rich creamy taste with just a little less zing.

MAKES 4 SERVINGS **PREPARATION TIME: 1 HOUR**

1 tablespoon olive oil
½ cup chopped onions
½ cup fresh or frozen corn kernels
¼ cup chopped red bell peppers
½ cup Vegetable Stock (page 45)
8 ounces Lightlife Quinoa Sesame
    Tempeh or any Lightlife tempeh
    products

2 teaspoons Ancho Chili Dry Rub
    (page 166)
Freshly ground black pepper
1 cup Tomato Chipotle "Cream"
    Sauce (page 77)
Eight 6-inch corn tortillas
6 ounces soy jalapeño Jack cheese,
    grated (approximately 1½ cups)

1. Preheat the oven to 350°F. In a nonstick skillet over medium heat, heat the olive oil. Add the onions and cook, stirring, for 2 to 3 minutes. Add the corn and bell peppers and cook, stirring, for 5 minutes more. Add ¼ cup of the vegetable stock and simmer for 4 to 5 minutes to reduce. Crumble the tempeh by hand and add to the skillet with the remaining ¼ cup of vegetable stock. Season with the ancho rub and black pepper.

2. Put a thin coating of the chipotle sauce on the bottom of a casserole dish. Steam or microwave the tortillas to soften and add approximately ¼ cup of the tempeh mixture and 2 tablespoons of cheese to the center of one tortilla. Roll tightly and place in casserole dish. Repeat this process for all the tortillas. Evenly spread the remainder of the sauce over the enchiladas and bake for 25 to 30 minutes.

Totally
dairy-free
cooking

✳ ROASTED PORTOBELLO AND SOY MOZZARELLA MELT

Texture, texture, texture. This sandwich is full of gooey soy cheese, and juicy, meaty mushrooms, layered between delicious crispy, toasted bread. Everyone in your family will enjoy this ultimate dairy-free delight.

CALORIES: 273.1	
FAT: 12.4G	
PROTEIN: 13.7G	
CARBOHYDRATE: 28.4G	
CHOLESTEROL: 1MG	
SODIUM: 680MG	

MAKES 4 SERVINGS　　　　　　**PREPARATION TIME: 30 MINUTES**

2 medium portobello mushrooms, stems trimmed, rinsed and patted dry
2 teaspoons extra-virgin olive oil
2 tablespoons balsamic vinegar
Sea salt and freshly ground black pepper

3 tablespoons Pumpkin Seed, Basil and Miso Pesto (page 172), or any other pesto from this book
8 slices spelt or 7-grain bread
6 ounces soy mozzarella, thinly sliced
4 slices ripe tomato
2 teaspoons soy margarine

Clean vegetables as you are getting ready to cook with them. Cleaning them too far in advance removes their natural preservatives and they begin to lose their essential vitamins and nutrients.

1. Preheat the oven to 350°F. Rub the mushrooms with the olive oil and vinegar. Season with salt and pepper.

2. Place the mushrooms flesh side down on a baking tray and roast for 10 to 12 minutes, or until soft. Thinly slice the mushrooms when they have cooled. Do not turn off the oven.

3. Spread the pesto on all 8 pieces of bread. Divide the mozzarella on 4 pieces of bread. Put the tomato slices on top of the cheese. Place the portobello slices on top of the tomato and put the remaining 4 slices of bread on top to complete the sandwiches.

4. Heat a medium nonstick skillet over medium heat. Melt the margarine. Add the sandwiches, 2 at a time, and cook until browned on one side (place a heavy object on top of each sandwich to help it brown evenly). Turn over and brown on the other side. Each side should take 2 to 3 minutes to brown. Place the sandwiches on a baking sheet and finish cooking in the oven for 5 minutes.

Vegetarian Dishes

✳ 109

✳ PORTOBELLO MUSHROOM FAJITAS

CALORIES: 221.2

FAT: 7.4G

PROTEIN: 5.4G

CARBOHYDRATE: 35.3G

CHOLESTEROL: 0MG

SODIUM: 174MG

Grilled or roasted portobello mushrooms have a meatlike texture and flavor. For a truly exquisite dining experience, drizzle a little white truffle oil over the mushrooms just before serving for an extra intense flavor sensation. Tofu Sour Cream (page 163), Roasted Corn–Chipotle Salsa (page 169) and Guacamole (page 161) are all excellent condiments for this dish.

MAKES 4 SERVINGS	PREPARATION TIME: 30 MINUTES

2 jumbo portobello mushrooms, stems trimmed, rinsed and patted dry

3 tablespoons balsamic vinegar

4 teaspoons extra-virgin olive oil

2 Bermuda onions, thinly sliced

2 medium red bell peppers, thinly crosscut

2 medium yellow bell peppers, thinly crosscut

¼ teaspoon chili powder

Sea salt and freshly ground black pepper

Four 8-inch flour tortillas

1. Rub both sides of the mushrooms with a little vinegar and olive oil. Toss the onions and peppers with the remaining vinegar and olive oil. Season with chili powder, and salt and pepper to taste.

2. Grill the mushrooms, onions, and peppers over medium heat on a nonstick grill pan, or an outdoor grill for 3 to 4 minutes per side. (A broiler works as a last resort.) Slice the mushrooms in ½-inch bias cuts and arrange the peppers and onions on top. Serve with warm folded flour tortillas.

Totally dairy-free cooking

110 ✳

✳ BROWN RICE, RED BEAN AND VEGETABLE "MEAT" LOAF

This "meat" loaf is enjoyable the next day as a sandwich or snack, so don't worry about leftovers. For a real treat, make the Basic Ketchup (page 165) or one of the barbecue sauces. Spread it right on top of the loaf after baking. Traditionally, we serve it warm with Rosemary Mushroom au Jus (page 146) or Tahini Sauce (page 162).

CALORIES: 286.9

FAT: 3.5G

PROTEIN: 14.8G

CARBOHYDRATE: 50.2G

CHOLESTEROL: 0MG

SODIUM: 508MG

MAKES 10 SERVINGS   **PREPARATION TIME: 1¼ HOURS**

2 teaspoons olive oil

½ teaspoon minced garlic

1 teaspoon minced shallots

1 cup chopped onions

½ cup chopped carrots

¼ cup chopped celery

¾ cup chopped bell peppers

3 spears asparagus, chopped

1 cup cooked textured vegetable protein (TVP)

¼ teaspoon dried oregano

¼ teaspoon dried thyme

¼ teaspoon dried basil

½ teaspoon ground cumin

3 tablespoons tamari soy sauce

¼ cup rice wine (*mirin*)

⅛ teaspoon freshly ground black pepper

4 cups cooked brown rice

2½ cups canned, drained red kidney beans

4 tablespoons egg whites (from about 2 eggs)

2 cups whole wheat bread crumbs

Sea salt

1. Preheat the oven to 325°F. In a large nonstick skillet over medium heat, heat the olive oil. Add the garlic, shallots and onions and cook, stirring, until the onions are translucent, 4 to 5 minutes. Add the carrots, celery, bell peppers and asparagus. Cook for an additional 3 to 4 minutes, then add the textured vegetable protein, oregano, thyme, basil, cumin, tamari, rice wine and black pepper. Cook, stirring, for 5 minutes more. Remove from the heat.

2. In a mixing bowl, combine the sautéed vegetables with the rice and beans, and mix well. Add the egg whites and bread crumbs and mix again. Season with salt to taste.

3. Spray a nonstick loaf pan with canola oil spray and put the mixture into the pan, pressing firmly to fill all the sides. Cover with foil and bake in the oven for 30 to 40 minutes, removing the foil cover for the last 10 minutes of cooking time. Let rest for 15 minutes before slicing.

Vegetarian Dishes

Millet is becoming an increasingly popular grain. Soya granules are another type of TVP (textured vegetable protein).

Sprinkle a little soy Parmesan on top before baking for a crustier and more flavorful topping. Serve with Tahini Sauce (page 162), Rosemary Mushroom au Jus (page 146) or Wild About Mushroom Sauce (page 143) for some delightful variations.

MAKES 8 SERVINGS **PREPARATION TIME: 1¼ HOURS**

When washing fruits and vegetables that you bought at the supermarket, use a good scrub brush and a mild natural soap, e.g., Dr. Bronner's, and warm water to remove all of the wax and preservatives.

1 cup millet

2 tablespoons tamari soy sauce

1½ cups soya granules

1 tablespoon olive oil

1 teaspoon minced garlic

1 teaspoon minced shallots

1 cup chopped onions

1 cup chopped zucchini

½ cup chopped bell peppers

½ cup white wine

1 teaspoon ground coriander

¼ cup julienned fresh basil

¼ cup minced fresh parsley

1 cup Oil-free Tamari Brown Rice
   (page 187) or 1 cup cooked brown
   rice with 2 teaspoons of tamari soy
   sauce

1½ cups cooked lentils, pureed

2 tablespoons egg whites (from
   about 1 egg)

Sea salt

Freshly ground black pepper

1. Simmer the millet in 2½ cups of water for 15 minutes. Remove from the heat, cover and let stand for 20 minutes. Fluff the millet with a fork before using.

2. Meanwhile, in another saucepan, bring 1 cup of water to a boil with the tamari soy sauce. Add the soya. Remove the pot from the heat, and let it sit covered for 10 minutes. Fluff the granules with a fork before using.

3. Preheat the oven to 350°F. In a nonstick skillet over medium heat, heat the olive oil. Add the garlic and shallots and cook, stirring, until golden, about 1 minute. Add the onions, zucchini and bell peppers and cook, stirring, for 4 to 6 minutes. Add the wine, coriander, basil and parsley. Simmer until the liquid is reduced 75 percent, 4 to 5 minutes. Transfer to a mixing bowl.

Totally
dairy-free
cooking

4. Add to the sautéed vegetables, the rice, lentils, soya, millet, and egg whites and season with salt and black pepper to taste. Mix thoroughly.

5. Spray a nonstick loaf pan with canola oil spray and firmly press the mixture into the pan. Bake for 30 to 40 minutes. Let cool for 20 to 30 minutes before slicing.

Vegetarian
Dishes

* THREE-GRAIN VEGETABLE BURGERS

CALORIES: 121.1

FAT: 2.5G

PROTEIN: 4.1G

CARBOHYDRATE: 20.6G

CHOLESTEROL: 0MG

SODIUM: 324MG

This is an all-purpose vegetable burger recipe. A lot of store-bought and restaurant veggie burgers still use cheese as a binder, but these stay together wonderfully without it. You can substitute brown rice or cooked TVP for one of the grains. Try serving these burgers with Basic Ketchup (page 165) or Tahini Sauce (page 162). Once you make them, they can be refrigerated for 2 to 3 days, or frozen in sealed zip-top bags for up to 2 months. If you freeze them, let the burgers thaw in the refrigerator for 6 hours before cooking them as normal.

MAKES 24 SERVINGS	PREPARATION TIME: 1 HOUR, PLUS 2 HOURS REFRIGERATION

1 cup cooked bulgur

1 cup cooked quinoa

2 cups cooked couscous

2 tablespoons olive oil

1 tablespoon minced garlic

1 tablespoon minced shallots

8 ounces button mushrooms, sliced

½ cup balsamic vinegar

¼ cup dry cooking sherry

1 cup canned or cooked chickpeas

1 cup minced onions

¾ cup minced carrots

1 tablespoon minced fresh tarragon

1 tablespoon minced fresh oregano,
   or ½ tablespoon dried

¼ cup minced fresh parsley

¼ cup egg whites (from about
   2 eggs)

2 cups whole wheat bread crumbs

1 tablespoon sea salt

½ teaspoon freshly ground black
   pepper

1. In a mixing bowl, mix together the bulgur, quinoa and couscous.

2. In a nonstick skillet over medium heat, heat 1 tablespoon of the olive oil. Add the garlic and shallots and cook, stirring, until golden, about 1 minute. Add the mushrooms and cook, stirring, for 5 minutes. Add the vinegar and sherry, and simmer for 3 to 4 minutes. Add the chickpeas, and stir. Transfer all of the ingredients to a food processor and puree.

3. In a nonstick skillet over medium heat, heat the remaining 1 tablespoon of olive oil. Add the onions and carrots and cook, stirring, until softened, 5 to 7 minutes.

Totally
dairy-free
cooking

114 *

4. In the mixing bowl with the grains, combine the chickpea puree and the carrot-onion mixture. Add the tarragon, oregano, parsley, egg whites and bread crumbs. Mix well and season with the salt and black pepper. Form into twenty-four 4-ounce balls. Hand press into patties. Refrigerate a minimum of 2 hours before cooking.

5. Spray a nonstick skillet with canola oil spray and set over low heat. Cook the patties for 3 to 4 minutes per side. (Place a light-weight object on top of the patties while cooking to give a uniform texture.)

✳ MILLET AND WILD MUSHROOM "MEAT" BALLS

CALORIES: 116.3
FAT: 1.7G
PROTEIN: 8.4G
CARBOHYDRATE: 19G
CHOLESTEROL: 0MG
SODIUM: 241MG

These "meat" balls have all of the texture of real meat because of the millet. They can be served with any pasta or even as an appetizer.

MAKES 16 SERVINGS   PREPARATION TIME: 1 HOUR, PLUS 2 HOURS REFRIGERATION

2 cups millet

2 tablespoons plus 2 teaspoons tamari soy sauce

1 cup soya granules

1 tablespoon olive oil

1 teaspoon minced garlic

½ cup chopped onions

½ cup chopped bell pepper

½ cup marsala wine

1½ cups chopped shiitake mushrooms

4 tablespoons egg whites (from about 2 eggs)

¼ cup minced fresh parsley

8 fresh basil leaves, julienned

1 teaspoon dried oregano

1 teaspoon sea salt

Freshly ground black pepper

½ cup whole wheat bread crumbs

1. Simmer the millet in 5 cups of water for 15 minutes. Remove from the heat, cover and let stand for 20 minutes. Fluff the millet with a fork before using. Meanwhile, in another saucepan bring 2 cups of water to a boil with 2 tablespoons of the tamari sauce. Add the soya. Remove the pot from the heat and let it sit covered for 10 minutes. Fluff with a fork before using.

2. Preheat the oven to 325°F. In a nonstick skillet over medium heat, heat the olive oil. Add the garlic and cook, stirring, until golden, about 1 minute. Add the onions and bell peppers and cook, stirring, for 3 minutes more. Add the marsala, the remaining 2 teaspoons tamari and the mushrooms. Simmer until the liquid has been reduced by 75 percent, 4 to 5 minutes. Transfer to a mixing bowl.

3. Add to the sautéed vegetables, the millet, soya, egg whites, parsley, basil and oregano and mix well with a plastic spatula. Season with the salt and pepper to taste. Form into 16 balls and dredge in the bread crumbs. Refrigerate for 2 hours to set.

4. Spray a nonstick baking tray with canola oil spray. Place the veggie balls evenly apart on the baking tray. Bake for 30 to 35 minutes, until golden brown.

Totally dairy-free Cooking

✳ TVP, SWEET POTATO AND BELL PEPPER CHILI

You won't have to call your local fire department to put out the fire after eating this delicious and mild chili. Try mixing in cooked brown rice when reheating. This chili is great with garnishes such as grated soy cheddar, Tofu Sour Cream (page 163) and sliced scallions, which can all be served in bowls on the side.

CALORIES: 144.5

FAT: 2.1G

PROTEIN: 7.3G

CARBOHYDRATE: 22.5G

CHOLESTEROL: 0MG

SODIUM: 320MG

MAKES 10 SERVINGS	PREPARATION TIME: 50 MINUTES, PLUS 1 TO 2 HOURS TO SOAK, AND 1 TO 2 HOURS TO SET

1 cup textured vegetable protein (TVP)

1 tablespoon tamari soy sauce

1 tablespoon olive oil

1 teaspoon minced garlic

1 teaspoon minced shallots

1 cup chopped onions

1½ cups peeled and diced sweet potatoes

½ cup fresh or frozen corn kernels

1 cup dry red wine

Two 14½-ounce cans diced tomatoes, drained

2 teaspoons chili powder

1 teaspoon ground cumin

1 teaspoon sea salt

¼ teaspoon freshly ground black pepper

1 cup diced bell pepper

1 tablespoon barley malt or molasses

Two 15-ounce cans kidney beans, rinsed and drained

1 tablespoon tomato paste

2 tablespoons minced fresh cilantro

1. In a mixing bowl, soak the textured vegetable protein in 1 cup of water and the tamari for 1 to 2 hours. Drain and set aside.

2. In a medium saucepan over medium heat, heat the olive oil. Add the garlic, shallots and onions and cook, stirring, until the onions are translucent, about 5 minutes. Add the sweet potatoes, corn and wine, and simmer for 10 minutes. Add the tomatoes, chili, cumin, salt and black pepper, and bring to a simmer. Add the drained TVP and bell pepper, and simmer 5 minutes more. Add the malt, beans and tomato paste, and simmer for 12 to 15 minutes. Remove from the heat, stir in the cilantro, then let sit for 1 to 2 hours for optimum flavors. Bring back to a simmer over medium heat before serving.

Vegetarian Dishes

✳ 117

✳ JOE'S VEGAN SPECIAL

CALORIES 167.4

FAT 3.8G

PROTEIN 22.4G

CARBOHYDRATE 15.6G

CHOLESTEROL 106MG

SODIUM 341MG

There was a series of Joe's and Original Joe's Restaurants in California in the '70s and '80s. They all had this Blue Plate Special on the menu using ground beef. (I've substituted TVP here, however.) It was a very popular meal whether you wanted breakfast, lunch or dinner because it was filling and satisfying. My mother would often replicate this classic dish for a quick and easy one-pan meal. (I guess it was her version of Hamburger Helper.) My dad always sprinkled grated cheddar cheese over his portion. For that extra treat, sprinkle some grated soy cheddar over yours.

If you don't want to use TVP, substitute ground free-range beef, chicken or turkey or even freshly ground tuna to make a more healthful meat version of this recipe. If you use meat, adjust the cooking time to ensure that the meat is properly cooked.

Tofu is available in three different varieties in the produce section of most supermarkets. Use firm or extra-firm tofu when frying or sautéing. Use soft or silken tofu for pureeing, vinaigrettes and making desserts.

MAKES 2 SERVINGS	PREPARATION TIME: 15 MINUTES

½ cup chopped onions

2 medium whole button mushrooms, sliced

1½ teaspoons tamari soy sauce

½ cup chopped frozen spinach

1 cup cooked textured vegetable protein (TVP)

1 large egg

1 large egg white

Sea salt and freshly ground black pepper

1. Heat a nonstick sauté pan over medium heat and spray with canola oil spray. Cook the onions, stirring, until golden, 2 to 3 minutes. Add the mushrooms and 1 teaspoon of the tamari. Continue to cook, stirring, for 2 to 3 minutes before adding the spinach. Cook, stirring, until the spinach is mixed in thoroughly. Remove from the pan and set aside.

2. Wipe the pan clean with paper towels and place back on the stovetop over medium heat. Spray with canola oil spray and add the TVP. Cook, stirring, for 2 minutes, then add the egg and egg white. Scramble for 1 to 2 minutes and add back the spinach-mushroom mixture and the remainder of the tamari. Cook until the eggs are done, about 3 minutes. Season with salt and pepper.

Totally
dairy-free
cooking

✳ BASIC VEGETABLE STIR-FRY

This is as basic as stir-fry gets. When preparing the vegetables, be sure to cut them all into a uniform size and shape for even cooking. Seasonal vegetables can be substituted for any one listed. Wok on the wild side—have fun and be creative. Serve with Oil-free Tamari Brown Rice (page 187) or Mango-Scallion Sticky Rice (page 188).

CALORIES: 98.1	
FAT: 2.8G	
PROTEIN: 2.9G	
CARBOHYDRATE: 14.8G	
CHOLESTEROL: 0MG	
SODIUM: 327MG	

MAKES 4 SERVINGS　　　　　　　　　　**PREPARATION TIME: 30 MINUTES**

2 teaspoons olive oil or sesame oil

1 cup diced taro root, or yuca root

½ cup diced carrots

½ cup chopped asparagus

1 cup chopped broccoli florets

1 cup diced zucchini

½ cup Stir-fry Sauce (page 154)

1 cup diced green or red bell
　peppers

3 tablespoons thinly sliced scallions

Freshly ground black pepper

In a nonstick wok over medium heat, heat the olive oil. Add the taro and cook, stirring, until slightly browned, 4 to 5 minutes. Add the carrots and asparagus and raise the heat to high. Cook, stirring, adding 1 tablespoon of water at a time (up to 4 tablespoons) to keep the vegetables from drying out, for 3 to 4 minutes. Add the broccoli and zucchini and cook, stirring, for an additional 2 to 3 minutes. Pour in the stir-fry sauce and add the bell peppers, and cook, stirring, 2 to 3 minutes, or until the vegetables are cooked through but still firm. Insert a fork into the middle of the taro root to check for doneness; it should go in easily. All other vegetables can be served at your desired firmness. Add the scallions and black pepper to taste.

To make your firm tofu extra firm, put it in the freezer for a couple of hours; take it out and wrap it in paper towels with a heavy object on top. As it defrosts, more of its liquid will run off, leaving the tofu even firmer and more like meat in texture.

Vegetarian
Dishes

✳ 119

We use only free-range meats and poultry in all of my restaurants. They taste better, they're more healthful and they are chemical- and drug-free. I recommend that you buy free-range chicken, turkey, and beef whenever possible. Aren't you worth it? In general, poultry is much leaner, is a better value and has less saturated fat than most other meats.

CALORIES: 423

FAT: 8.4G

PROTEIN: 29.7G

CARBOHYDRATE: 56.7G

CHOLESTEROL: 49MG

SODIUM: 281MG

This is a hearty burrito that will satisfy anyone's craving for real Mexican cuisine. Two tablespoons of soy cheddar or jalapeño Jack cheese can be sprinkled over the rice and bean mixture before rolling the chicken into the tortilla. You can replace the chicken with Seared Asian Tofu (page 184) or just have the beans and rice straight up for a vegetarian variation. To finish off your presentation, try serving with Guacamole (page 161) and Tofu Sour Cream (page 163).

MAKES 4 SERVINGS   **PREPARATION TIME: 40 MINUTES**

1 tablespoon olive oil

1 teaspoon minced garlic

¼ cup chopped onions

¼ cup chopped red bell peppers

½ cup chopped zucchini

2 cups cooked brown rice

1 cup cooked or canned black beans

1 tablespoon minced fresh cilantro

2 teaspoons ground chili powder

1 teaspoon ground coriander

½ teaspoon ground cumin

¼ teaspoon freshly ground black pepper, plus additional for seasoning chicken

1 teaspoon sea salt, plus additional for seasoning chicken

2 boneless skinless chicken breasts, pounded thin

Four 8- to 10-inch flour tortillas

4 tablespoons salsa, such as Roasted Corn–Chipotle (page 169)

1. Heat the olive oil in a nonstick skillet over medium heat. Add the garlic and onions and cook, stirring, until the onions are translucent, about 3 minutes. Add the bell peppers and zucchini and cook, stirring, until the vegetables are softened, about 5 minutes. Add the rice and beans, and stir. Season with the cilantro, chili powder, coriander, cumin, ¼ teaspoon of the black pepper and 1 teaspoon of the salt.

2. Rub the chicken breasts with salt and pepper. On an outdoor grill, or in a nonstick grill pan or skillet, sear or grill the chicken for 3 to 4 minutes on each side. Cut the chicken into ½-inch slices. Reserve for later.

Totally dairy-free Cooking

3. Preheat the oven to 300°F. Warm the tortillas for 2 minutes to make them more pliable, then remove from the oven and raise the oven temperature to 375°F. Store the tortillas under a hot damp towel to keep moist.

4. Lay a tortilla on a flat surface and put one quarter of the rice/bean mixture across the tortilla about 3 inches from the bottom. Leave 1½ inches on each side of the tortilla visible (this makes rolling the burrito easier). Lay a quarter of the sliced chicken breasts in the center of the rice/bean mixture. Spoon 1 tablespoon of salsa over the chicken. Fold in the sides of the tortilla and roll tightly. Seal the top of the tortilla with a spritz of warm water. Repeat this process with the three remaining tortillas.

5. Wrap each burrito in foil and warm in the oven for 10 to 12 minutes. They can also be microwaved (do not use foil) for 2 to 3 minutes on medium. Slice in half before serving.

Chicken,
turkey and
Duck

CALORIES: 617

FAT: 18.7G

PROTEIN: 88.4G

CARBOHYDRATE: 23.9G

CHOLESTEROL: 165MG

SODIUM: 1068MG

This phenomenal recipe will fool any die-hard Italian food lover into thinking it's the full-dairy version. For a gourmet treat, try placing a layer of sautéed spinach on the chicken breast before topping it with tomato sauce and soy cheeses. As a side dish, try serving Steamed Broccoli in Basil, White Wine and Garlic Broth (page 185).

MAKES 4 SERVINGS **PREPARATION TIME: 30 MINUTES**

Chicken should be vibrant in color with translucent meat when you buy it in the store. It is better to buy a whole bird and have it butchered fresh, using the different parts for different recipes. It's more cost effective. Don't forget to save the bones for making delicious homemade stock.

4 boneless, skinless chicken breasts, pounded thin (about 1½ pounds)
Sea salt and freshly ground black pepper
2 tablespoons egg whites (from about 1 egg)
¼ cup whole wheat bread crumbs

2 teaspoons olive oil
1 cup California Plum Tomato, Basil and Garlic Sauce (page 74), or ½ cup canned tomatoes
1 cup grated soy mozzarella, (about 4 ounces)
2 tablespoons grated soy Parmesan

1. Preheat the oven to 350°F. Season the chicken breasts with salt and pepper and cover with the egg whites. Sprinkle bread crumbs evenly on both sides.

2. In a nonstick skillet over medium heat, heat the olive oil. Add the chicken and cook until lightly browned on both sides, 2 to 3 minutes per side, but do not cook all the way through.

3. In a shallow casserole dish, spread ½ cup of the tomato sauce on the bottom and place the chicken on top. Pour the remaining ½ cup of the tomato sauce over the top. Evenly sprinkle the mozzarella and Parmesan over the sauce and breasts.

4. Bake for 8 to 10 minutes, or until the mozzarella is melted.

Totally
dairy-free
cooking

✳ CHICKEN FAJITAS WITH CILANTRO-WALNUT PESTO

Make a variety of condiments like Guacamole (page 161), Tofu Sour Cream (page 163), Three-Pepper Salsa (page 170) and Roasted Corn–Chipolte Salsa (page 169) to give this succulent dish a traditional and tasty flavor. To give your family a choice, try replacing the chicken with duck breasts, swordfish, tuna or grilled seasonal vegetables.

CALORIES: 412.9

FAT: 8.2G

PROTEIN: 38.4G

CARBOHYDRATE: 46.8G

CHOLESTEROL: 79MG

SODIUM: 365MG

MAKES 4 SERVINGS   PREPARATION TIME: 40 MINUTES, PLUS 2 TO 24 HOURS MARINATION

4 boneless, skinless chicken breasts, pounded thin (about 1½ pounds)

1 tablespoon Ancho Chili Dry Rub (page 166) or a mix of salt, freshly ground pepper and chili powder

2 tablespoons olive oil

6 slices Bermuda onion

2 red bell peppers, thinly sliced crosswise

2 yellow bell peppers, thinly sliced crosswise

4 teaspoons Cilantro-Walnut Pesto (page 171)

Sea salt and freshly ground black pepper

Four 8-inch whole wheat flour tortillas, warmed

1 lime, cut into 4 wedges

1. In a mixing bowl, rub the chicken with the Ancho Rub and olive oil and let sit in the refrigerator from 2 to 24 hours.

2. On an outdoor grill or in nonstick grill pan, cook the chicken over medium heat for 3 to 4 minutes on each side. Grill the onion and bell peppers for 3 to 4 minutes, tossing frequently.

3. Preheat the oven to 350°F. Heat the tortillas for 2 to 3 minutes or in the microwave for 30 seconds. Spread one teaspoon of the pesto over each cooked chicken breast and slice. Season with salt and pepper to taste. Place one sliced breast on each warm plate to serve. Add equal amounts of the onion and peppers on top. Serve with one warmed folded flour tortilla and a lime wedge, with a damp towel over the top to keep the tortilla moist.

Chicken, turkey and Duck

✱ CHICKEN SCARPARIELLO WITH SAUTÉED SPINACH

CALORIES: 267.7

FAT: 5.9G

PROTEIN: 41.5G

CARBOHYDRATE: 5.8G

CHOLESTEROL: 102MG

SODIUM: 197MG

No bones about it . . . or skin for that matter. This is a more healthful and quicker version of the Italian classic.

MAKES 4 SERVINGS	PREPARATION TIME: 30 MINUTES

4 boneless, skinless chicken breasts pounded thin (about 1½ pounds)

2 tablespoons spelt flour or whole wheat flour

Sea salt and freshly ground black pepper

2 teaspoons olive oil

4 cloves garlic, thinly sliced

½ pound of precooked chicken sausage, sliced (about 2 medium sausages)

2 tablespoons balsamic vinegar

½ cup dry red wine

½ cup Roasted Chicken Stock (page 40) or low-sodium canned stock

¼ cup julienned basil leaves

2 bunches whole spinach leaves, rinsed and dried

1. Dredge the chicken in the flour and season with salt and pepper.

2. In a nonstick skillet over medium heat, heat the olive oil. Add the garlic and cook, stirring, until golden, about 1 minute. Add the sausage and brown for 2 minutes, stirring. Add the breasts and brown on one side for 2 to 3 minutes. Turn over the breasts and add the vinegar and wine to deglaze the pan. Cook for 2 to 3 minutes or until the liquid is reduced by half. Add the chicken stock and basil. Simmer the chicken for an additional 3 to 4 minutes or until cooked through. Remove the chicken and keep warm. Then add the spinach to the remaining sauce in the skillet. Toss for 2 to 3 minutes or until cooked and season with salt and pepper to taste. Remove from the heat.

3. Arrange equal amounts of spinach on 4 plates. Place a whole chicken breast on each spinach bed and place the sausage and garlic over it. Then pour the pan sauce over the breasts.

Totally dairy-free cooking

✳ MARGARITA CHICKEN PAILLARD

This is the ultimate summer dish, although it's guaranteed not to make you drunk except maybe from happiness. The acid from the lime juice and the alcohol from the tequila break down the muscle tissue in the chicken to make this one of the most tender chicken dishes you'll ever eat. Serve the breasts whole with Tomato Basil Concasse (page 151) or Mango, Tomato and Black Bean Salsa (page 153). Try it over the Chopped Vegetable, Tofu and Romaine Salad (page 69) or Mesclun Greens with Balsamic Mustard Vinaigrette (page 68).

CALORIES: 286.7

FAT: 5.6G

PROTEIN: 39.7G

CARBOHYDRATE: 8.2G

CHOLESTEROL: 99MG

SODIUM: 113MG

MAKES 4 SERVINGS   PREPARATION TIME: 30 MINUTES, PLUS 2 TO 24 HOURS MARINATION

1 tablespoon olive oil

Juice of 2 limes

3 tablespoons Triple Sec

2 tablespoons tequila

1 tablespoon minced fresh cilantro

2 teaspoons seeded and minced
  jalapeño pepper, optional

4 boneless, skinless chicken breasts,
  pounded thin (about 1½ pounds)

Sea salt and freshly ground black
  pepper

1. In a mixing bowl, combine the olive oil, lime juice, Triple Sec, tequila, cilantro and jalapeño, if desired. Season the chicken with salt and black pepper and place in the marinade. Cover and refrigerate for 2 to 24 hours. Marinate for as long as possible to create "a melt in your mouth" texture.

2. On an outdoor grill or in a nonstick grill pan over medium heat, grill the marinated chicken for 2 to 4 minutes on each side, depending on thickness.

Chicken,
turkey and
Duck

✳ 129

✳ CITRUS-ROSEMARY ROASTED CHICKEN

CALORIES: 224.9

FAT: 5G

PROTEIN: 36.8G

CARBOHYDRATE: 6.4G

CHOLESTEROL: 112MG

SODIUM: 120MG

Chicken can sometimes get dried out when you roast it, so to avoid making that mistake, make sure the bird is at room temperature when you put it into the oven. Serve with Three-Potato Mash (page 100), Oven-Baked Spiced Yuca Fries (page 191), Soy Creamed Spinach (page 178) or Taboule (page 64). The Roasted Garlic au Jus (page 145) goes perfectly with this dish. For the leftovers the next day, try one of my homemade barbecue sauces as a dipping sauce.

MAKES 4 SERVINGS	PREPARATION TIME: 1¼ HOURS, PLUS 1 HOUR MARINATION

1 medium juice orange

½ medium yellow onion, chopped

5 cloves garlic, halved

2 teaspoons minced fresh rosemary

2 teaspoons kosher salt

1 teaspoon freshly ground black pepper

One 3½- to 4-pound chicken, washed and dried

1. Remove the zest from the orange, then peel and chop the orange into approximately 16 pieces. In a mixing bowl, toss the orange with the onion, garlic, 1 teaspoon of the rosemary, 1 teaspoon of the salt and ½ teaspoon of the pepper. Stuff the mixture into the cavity of the chicken.

2. In a small bowl, mix together the orange zest and remaining 1 teaspoon rosemary, 1 teaspoon salt and ½ teaspoon pepper. Lifting the skin carefully, hand rub this mixture into the breast and thigh meat of the chicken and let sit for up to 1 hour.

3. When marination is almost done, preheat the oven to 350°F. Roast the chicken for 1 hour, or until the juice is clear when the thigh is poked. Let rest for 15 minutes before carving. Remove the skin before serving.

Totally
dairy-free
Cooking

✳ SEARED BREAST OF DUCK WITH PEAR, GINGER AND PORT SAUCE

This is a great dish for the fall. It's satisfying and high in flavor. Most people think duck is fatty, but this recipe is a wonderful healthful way to enjoy a rich and flavorful duck meal. You can substitute chicken breasts for the duck if you prefer. Serve it with the Mashed Sweet Potatoes (page 181) and the Slow-Cooked String Beans (page 189) for a night to remember!

CALORIES: 501	
FAT: 11.1G	
PROTEIN: 35.5G	
CARBOHYDRATE: 58G	
CHOLESTEROL: 12MG	
SODIUM: 143MG	

MAKES 4 SERVINGS   **PREPARATION TIME: 30 MINUTES**

1¼ pounds boneless, skinless duck
   breasts
Sea salt and freshly ground black
   pepper
1 teaspoon ground coriander
2 teaspoons olive oil
4 teaspoons minced shallots
10 to 12 thin slices fresh ginger

½ cup port wine
½ cup fresh pear juice, or cider
1 cup Duck Stock (page 43) or
   Roasted Chicken Stock (page 41)
¼ cup fresh orange juice (from about
   1 orange)
2 teaspoons arrowroot

> When handling poultry, to avoid any cross-contamination clean your cutting board, knives and hands thoroughly with an antibacterial soap.

1. Remove all fat from the duck. Sprinkle salt, pepper and the coriander on both sides of the breasts.

2. Heat the olive oil in a nonstick skillet over medium heat. Add the duck and brown, about 3 minutes on each side. Remove the breasts from the pan and set aside.

3. In the same skillet over medium heat, cook the shallots and ginger, stirring, until golden, about 2 minutes. Add the wine to deglaze the pan. Add the pear juice, stock and orange juice, and stir. Place the breasts back into sauce and cook until the liquid is reduced by half. This should take 8 to 10 minutes. Remove the duck when cooked medium.

4. In a small bowl, mix together the arrowroot with 4 teaspoons of cold water, and add to the sauce. Simmer 2 to 3 minutes more and strain the sauce. Thinly slice the duck breasts against the grain and serve the sauce over the top.

Chicken, turkey and Duck

CALORIES: 89.8

FAT: 2.7G

PROTEIN: 10.7G

CARBOHYDRATE: 5.1G

CHOLESTEROL: 28MG

SODIUM: 198MG

Whenever you go to the store and buy ground turkey, it's almost entirely dark meat and end products. This recipe calls for both dark meat and light meat. Ask your butcher to grind you some white meat to go with the dark. You might pay a little more, but you're going to get a more healthful, better tasting turkey meatball. Try them with the California Plum Tomato, Basil and Garlic Sauce (page 74).

MAKES 10 SERVINGS   **PREPARATION TIME: 40 MINUTES**

1 tablespoon freshly grated
   horseradish

1 tablespoon Worcestershire sauce

1 tablespoon tamari soy sauce

2 tablespoons minced fresh parsley

2 tablespoons minced shallots

1 large egg white

5 fresh basil leaves, julienned

½ cup whole wheat bread crumbs

8 ounces ground turkey breast

8 ounces ground turkey dark meat

Sea salt and freshly ground black
   pepper

1. Preheat the oven to 350°F. In a medium bowl, thoroughly mix all of the ingredients together and season with salt and black pepper. Divide the mixture into 10 balls (use a ¼-cup measure to gauge approximate size). Hand-roll the balls and place on a nonstick baking tray.

2. Bake the meatballs for 18 to 20 minutes.

NOTES: Double the recipe and make into a 9 x 5-inch meat loaf and bake for 45 to 50 minutes. Serve with Roasted Garlic au Jus (page 145).

Totally
dairy-free
cooking

✳ SOUTHWESTERN TURKEY LOAF

This meat loaf comes out juicy and packs a lot of flavor. You won't need any sauce or condiments with this dish. For an occasional twist, add ½ cup of grated soy cheddar to the center of the loaf before baking.

CALORIES: 202.6	
FAT: 7.9G	
PROTEIN: 26.5G	
CARBOHYDRATE: 26.4G	
CHOLESTEROL: 55MG	
SODIUM: 91MG	

MAKES 10 SERVINGS   **PREPARATION TIME: 1 HOUR, PLUS 10 TO 15 MINUTES TO REST**

1 tablespoon olive oil
1 teaspoon minced garlic
1 teaspoon minced shallots
1 cup chopped onions
½ cup fresh or frozen corn kernels
½ cup chopped red or yellow bell peppers
1 tablespoon minced fresh cilantro
1 tablespoon coarsely ground mustard

1 teaspoon chili powder
1 teaspoon ground cumin
1 teaspoon ground coriander
Sea salt and freshly ground black pepper
1 pound ground turkey breast
1 pound ground turkey dark meat
2 tablespoons egg whites (from about 1 egg)
1 cup whole wheat bread crumbs

1. Preheat the oven to 350°F. In a nonstick skillet over medium heat, heat the olive oil. Add the garlic and shallots and cook, stirring, until golden, about 1 minute. Add the onions and continue to cook, stirring, until the onions are translucent, 3 to 4 minutes. Add the corn and bell peppers and cook, stirring, for an additional 3 to 4 minutes. Add a couple of tablespoons of stock or water, if necessary, to keep the ingredients from sticking to the pan. Season with the cilantro, mustard, chili powder, cumin, coriander and salt and black pepper to taste. Set aside to cool.

2. In a mixing bowl, mix together the ground turkey, egg whites and bread crumbs. Add the cooled vegetable mixture and blend thoroughly. Add salt and black pepper if desired.

3. Press the turkey mixture into a nonstick loaf pan. Press lightly with a spatula to fill in evenly. Bake for 50 minutes or until the juices run clear. Let rest for 10 to 15 minutes before slicing.

It pays to be friends with your butcher. Commercial ground turkey and chicken are full of end products and are mostly dark meat. Ask your butcher what the percentage of dark to light meat is in his ground meat. Ask him to grind it for you fresh and get 50 percent dark and 50 percent white meat. This way your cooked meat will not be too dry or filled with end products you don't want.

Chicken, turkey and Duck

✳ 133

CALORIES: 159.7

FAT: 4.5G

PROTEIN: 24G

CARBOHYDRATE: 16G

CHOLESTEROL: 54MG

SODIUM: 332MG

Ground chicken isn't a typical way to make a meat loaf, but this recipe will convince you that you've been missing out on something terrific. As a time saver, ask your butcher to freshly grind the chicken for you. Horseradish adds a unique, zesty flavor that will keep your family and guests wondering, "What is that spice?" Serve with Roasted Garlic au Jus (page 145), or with Josie's Barbecue Sauce (page 167) as a dipping sauce as a change of flavor for leftovers.

MAKES 8 SERVINGS   **PREPARATION TIME: 1 HOUR**

1 pound ground chicken breasts

1 pound ground chicken dark meat

1 tablespoon minced garlic

1 tablespoon minced shallots

1 tablespoon freshly grated
  horseradish

1 teaspoon Worcestershire sauce

2 tablespoons tamari soy sauce

3 tablespoons rice wine (*mirin*)

2 tablespoons egg whites (from
  about 1 egg)

Sea salt

¼ teaspoon freshly ground black
  pepper

1 teaspoon chopped fresh oregano,
  or ½ teaspoon dried

1 teaspoon chopped fresh thyme, or
  ½ teaspoon dried

1 teaspoon chopped fresh sage, or
  ½ teaspoon dried

½ cup whole wheat bread crumbs

¼ cup chopped fresh parsley

1. Preheat the oven to 375°F. In a mixing bowl, mix all the ingredients together thoroughly.

2. Press the chicken mixture into a loaf pan sprayed with canola oil spray. Press lightly with a spatula to fill in evenly. Bake in the oven for 40 to 50 minutes, until cooked through. Let cool for 10 to 15 minutes before slicing.

Totally
daiRy-free
CookinG

I have provided more healthful versions of all the condiments, sauces and side dishes usually served with your turkey on Thanksgiving, so I wanted to include my favorite recipe to cook your Turkey Day bird. For a real traditional meal, serve the turkey with my Apple Cranberry Chutney (page 164), Mashed Sweet Potatoes (page 181), Slow-Cooked String Beans (page 189), Spiced Sweet Potato and Cranberry Couscous (page 191), Three-Potato Mash (page 180), and Spiced Pumpkin–Tofu Pie (page 224). No one but you will know you've made an entire Thanksgiving feast without any dairy! I know it's a long day of cooking but it only comes once a year, so enjoy it.

CALORIES: 78.9

FAT: 1.7G

PROTEIN: 1.6G

CARBOHYDRATE: 7.5G

CHOLESTEROL: 2MG

SODIUM: 37MG

MAKES 10 SERVINGS   **PREPARATION TIME: 2½ HOURS**

3 cups chopped carrots

2 cups chopped celery

2 cups chopped onions

1 head garlic, halved

2 cups dry white wine

One 10- to 12-pound turkey breast,
   on the bone, fresh or thawed

1 tablespoon olive oil

Sea salt and freshly ground black
   pepper

1. Preheat the oven to 375°F. In a large roasting pan, add the carrots, celery, onions, garlic and wine. Place the bird on top of the vegetables. Rub the breasts with the olive oil and season liberally with salt and pepper.

2. Roast for approximately 1 hour and 50 minutes or until the interior temperature reaches 130°F. Remove from the oven and let rest 30 minutes. Remove both sides of the breast from the carcass and set aside to serve after you have prepared the gravy. Don't throw away the vegetables or carcass—you will need these for preparing Turkey Stock and Thanksgiving Gravy (see pages 136 and 137).

Chicken, turkey and DUCK

✳ TURKEY STOCK

PER CUP	
CALORIES: 50	
FAT: 1.6G	
PROTEIN: 6.2G	
CARBOHYDRATE: 3.8G	
CHOLESTEROL: 37MG	
SODIUM: 59MG	

Roasting the bones of the turkey gives the stock a fuller richer flavor and eliminates most of the excess fat.

MAKES ABOUT 5 CUPS   **PREPARATION TIME: 2 HOURS**

Leftover vegetables from
    Thanksgiving Turkey (page 135)

1 cup dry sherry
1 turkey carcass

1. Fill a large stockpot with 12 cups of filtered water and add the vegetables.

2. Heat the Thanksgiving Turkey roasting pan on the stove top and add the sherry, stirring briefly, to deglaze the pan. Add the drippings to the stockpot.

3. Break up the carcass and remove any excess fat. Put the broken up carcass into the stockpot and bring it to a boil. Reduce the heat and simmer uncovered for about 1 hour and 40 minutes.

4. Strain the stock through a fine-mesh strainer or cheesecloth.

Totally
dairy-free
cooking

✳ THANKSGIVING GRAVY

Even if you overcook your turkey, this gravy is guaranteed to save the day. And since it's a more healthful version than the classic, go ahead and splurge!

PER ¼ CUP

CALORIES: 88.6

FAT: 3G

PROTEIN: 7.6G

CARBOHYDRATE: 3.9G

CHOLESTEROL: 21MG

SODIUM: 23MG

MAKES 4 CUPS   **PREPARATION TIME: 45 MINUTES**

2 teaspoons olive oil

2 tablespoons minced shallots

1 cup chopped onions

½ cup chopped carrots

½ cup dry cooking sherry

½ cup dry white wine

5 fresh sage leaves, minced

5 fresh tarragon leaves, minced

5 cups Turkey Stock (page 136), fat
  removed

1 tablespoon arrowroot

Sea salt and freshly ground black
  pepper

1. In medium saucepan over medium heat, heat the olive oil. Add the shallots and cook, stirring, until golden, about 2 minutes. Add the onions and cook, stirring, until translucent, 3 to 5 minutes.

2. Add the carrots, sherry and wine. Bring to a boil, then reduce the heat and simmer until reduced by 75 percent, 4 to 5 minutes. Add the sage, tarragon and turkey stock. Bring to boil again, then reduce the heat and simmer for about 25 minutes more.

3. Turn off the heat, puree with an electric handheld blender or in a food processor.

4. In a small bowl, mix the arrowroot with 2 tablespoons of cold water and add to the gravy. Simmer an additional 10 minutes. For a smoother texture, strain the gravy through a mesh strainer. Season with salt and pepper to taste.

Chicken,
turkey and
Duck

✳ 137

If David Letterman had a top 1001 list, you still wouldn't be able to find all of the uses for the recipes in this chapter. Have some fun experimenting with all the variations you can discover. These sauces are great with fish, chicken, vegetables and even rice! So get creative and see if you can invent your own masterpiece! I've offered several ideas on unique ways to use these sauces throughout the book, but don't feel limited to my suggestions.

✳ BRANDY SHALLOT AND GREEN PEPPERCORN "CREAM" SAUCE

The essence of brandy combined with the spiciness of shallots and peppercorns make this "cream" sauce taste incredible. Its robust flavor will enhance any meal. Try it with the Seared Yellowfin Tuna Burger (page 98). It's also great with poultry and filet mignon. For a more pure and full flavor substitute beef or chicken stock, to match the meat you're serving.

MAKES 2 CUPS	PREPARATION TIME: 40 MINUTES

Once open, a box of soy milk will be good in the refrigerator for ten days. When you first open the box, pour out two ounces into a separate glass so that you can reshut it and give it a good shake.

1 tablespoon olive oil
1 tablespoon minced shallots
½ teaspoon minced garlic
¼ cup brandy
2 cups Vegetable Stock (page 45), or
   Roasted Chicken Stock (page 40)
4 fresh sage leaves
2 teaspoons Worcestershire sauce

1 teaspoon sea salt
⅛ teaspoon freshly ground black
   pepper
2 tablespoons green peppercorns
   (canned in brine)
½ cup plain soy milk
2 tablespoons arrowroot
1 tablespoon soy margarine

1. In a medium saucepan, heat the olive oil over medium heat. Add the shallot and garlic and cook until golden, about 2 minutes. Add the brandy and cook until reduced to an essence, about 2 minutes. Add the stock and bring to a simmer. Add the sage, Worcestershire, salt, pepper, peppercorns and soy milk. Reduce the heat and simmer for 10 to 12 minutes. A light peppery flavor will develop and the richness of the brandy will be evident.

2. In a small mixing bowl, mix the arrowroot with 2 tablespoons of water. Add the arrowroot mixture and margarine to the sauce. Let simmer for 3 to 5 minutes. Remove the sage leaves before serving. This can be stored, covered, in the refrigerator for up to 3 days.

Totally dairy-free cooking

✳ WILD ABOUT MUSHROOM SAUCE

If you're feeling a bit wild, then this is the sauce for you. It's perfect with seared snapper, tilapia or chicken. Truffle oil gives that special finish that will intrigue your guests and dazzle their taste buds. Truffle oil can be found in specialty grocery stores, especially the Italian ones. Remember to keep the truffle oil (and all oils) in a cool dark place.

PER ¼ CUP

CALORIES: 68.5

FAT: 5.1G

PROTEIN: 1.3G

CARBOHYDRATE: 5.1G

CHOLESTEROL: 0MG

SODIUM: 208MG

MAKES 3 CUPS   **PREPARATION TIME: 40 MINUTES**

3 ounces shiitake mushrooms

3 ounces cremini mushrooms

3 ounces portobello mushrooms

Sea salt and freshly ground black
    pepper

1 teaspoon chopped fresh tarragon

2 tablespoons chopped fresh basil

¼ cup balsamic vinegar

1½ cups Vegetable Stock (page 45)

1 tablespoon white truffle olive oil

3 tablespoons extra-virgin olive oil

1. Preheat the oven to 350°F. Clean, slice and season the mushrooms with salt and pepper to taste. Roast on a sheet pan with foil to cover for 18 to 20 minutes. Let cool for 10 minutes.

2. Place the mushrooms in a food processor with the tarragon, basil, vinegar and bouillon, and process. Season with salt and pepper. While the processor is on, slowly drizzle in the truffle oil and olive oil. Heat the sauce briefly in a small saucepan on medium-low heat before serving. Store, covered, in the refrigerator for up to 3 days.

ʃAUces

✳ ROASTED TOMATO AND WHITE TRUFFLE COULIS

PER ¼ CUP

CALORIES: 100.4

FAT: 7.8G

PROTEIN: 2.3G

CARBOHYDRATE: 6.6G

CHOLESTEROL: 0MG

SODIUM: 112MG

White truffle olive oil is an important ingredient in this sauce. The intense earthy flavor is spectacular. Most gourmet food stores, especially Italian specialty food shops, should carry this oil. Serve this with the Steamed Yukon Potatoes and Broccoli Dumplings (page 33). It's also excellent served over your favorite tofu raviolis or small shell pasta.

MAKES 2 CUPS　　　　　　　　　　　　　　**PREPARATION TIME: 45 MINUTES**

12 whole canned plum tomatoes
　　(14½-ounce can)
1 teaspoon minced garlic
3 tablespoons extra-virgin olive oil
1 tablespoon [infused] white truffle
　　olive oil

1 teaspoon minced fresh basil
1 teaspoon minced fresh oregano
1 teaspoon sea salt
Freshly ground black pepper
½ cup Vegetable Stock (page 45)
½ cup soft tofu

1. Preheat the oven to 325°F. In a small Pyrex baking dish, mix together the tomatoes, garlic and 1 tablespoon olive oil. Roast for about 30 minutes.

2. Transfer the tomatoes to a food processor and add the remaining 2 tablespoons olive oil, the truffle oil, herbs, sea salt, pepper to taste, stock and tofu. Process to combine.

3. Heat the sauce briefly in a small saucepan over medium-low heat before serving. Store, covered, in the refrigerator for up to 3 days.

Totally
dairy-free
cooking

✳ ROASTED GARLIC AU JUS

With the perfect hint of roasted garlic, this sauce is a simple classic. I like to use this when I make Citrus–Rosemary Roasted Chicken (page 130). You can substitute beef stock if you're cooking a roast.

PER ¼ CUP

CALORIES: 61.6

FAT: 0.7G

PROTEIN: 9.6G

CARBOHYDRATE: 4.4G

CHOLESTEROL: 0MG

SODIUM: 467MG

MAKES 1¾ CUPS   **PREPARATION TIME: 1½ HOURS**

1 whole head garlic

1 teaspoon extra-virgin olive oil

1½ quarts Roasted Chicken Stock (page 40)

1 tablespoon tomato paste

2 teaspoons rice wine (*mirin*)

½ teaspoon Worcestershire sauce

1 teaspoon minced fresh parsley

2 tablespoons arrowroot

Sea salt and freshly ground black pepper

1. Preheat the oven to 350°F. Cut the whole head of garlic in half crosswise. Put the head back together, rub the outside with the olive oil, and cover with aluminum foil. Roast for 45 minutes. Let cool, unwrap, and squeeze out the garlic "meat."

2. Meanwhile, in a medium stockpot, bring the chicken stock to a boil, reduce the heat and simmer until the stock is reduced by 40 percent, about 1 hour.

3. Add the garlic "meat," tomato paste, wine, Worcestershire and parsley to the stock. Simmer for an additional 15 minutes.

4. In a small bowl, mix together the arrowroot and water with 2 tablespoons cold water. Add to the sauce and whisk for 2 minutes before serving. Season with sea salt and black pepper to taste. Store, covered, in the refrigerator for up to 3 days.

> When reheating your sauces, they should be brought up to a temperature high enough to kill any bacteria that might have grown.

SAUCES

✳ ROSEMARY MUSHROOM AU JUS

This is a great vegetarian sauce that can be served with vegetable meat loaf and is delicious on seared tofu. It can even be used as a stir-fry sauce for tofu, tempeh, seitan and your favorite vegetables. If you're using it with chicken, I suggest replacing the water with chicken stock for a richer poultry flavor.

MAKES 2 CUPS   **PREPARATION TIME: 40 MINUTES**

Like stocks and soups, never put a sauce in a sealed container in the refrigerator while it is hot because the heat will have no place to go and will cause the sauce to spoil faster.

½ tablespoon olive oil
½ tablespoon minced garlic
1 cup chopped onions
¼ pound button mushrooms, sliced (about 1 cup)
¼ teaspoon dried rosemary
⅛ teaspoon dried oregano
⅛ teaspoon dried thyme

¼ teaspoon ground coriander
¼ teaspoon sea salt
¼ teaspoon freshly ground black pepper
5 teaspoons tamari soy sauce
5 teaspoons rice wine (*mirin*)
2½ tablespoons arrowroot

1. Heat the olive oil in a nonstick skillet over medium heat. Add the garlic and onions and cook, stirring, until the onions are translucent, about 3 minutes. Add the mushrooms and cook, stirring, for 5 to 7 minutes more or until the mushrooms are tender. Add the dried herbs, salt and pepper.

2. In a saucepan, combine 3 cups water, the tamari and wine. Bring to a simmer and add ingredients from the skillet. Simmer for 10 minutes.

3. In a small bowl, stir together the arrowroot with 2½ tablespoons water, then add to the simmering sauce. Cook, stirring, for 2 to 3 minutes. Store, covered, in the refrigerator for up to 3 days.

Totally dairy-free cooking

✳ MISO BASIL LIME PESTO

Miso adds saltiness and smoothness to this twist on traditional pesto. It's garlic free and lower in fat because I use less oil than a regular pesto recipe usually calls for. It's important to use the mellower flavored misos rather than traditional red miso which would overpower the milder flavor of the basil and cashews. I suggest using 1 tablespoon of pesto per 1 cup cooked pasta. This pesto is also great dolloped on grilled or sautéed fish and chicken.

PER 2 TABLESPOONS
CALORIES: 29.3
FAT: 1.8G
PROTEIN: 1.1G
CARBOHYDRATE: 2.9G
CHOLESTEROL: 0MG
SODIUM: 43MG

MAKES 1 CUP **PREPARATION TIME: 30 MINUTES**

¼ cup whole cashews

Juice of 1 lime

1 cup packed fresh basil leaves

1 tablespoon barley miso, or
  chickpea miso

⅛ teaspoon salt

¼ teaspoon freshly ground black
  pepper

1 tablespoon olive oil

1. Preheat the oven to 350°F. Toast the cashews on a baking sheet for 5 minutes. Set aside to cool.

2. Combine all the ingredients, except the olive oil and cashews, in a food processor. Add 1 tablespoon of water and pulse to mix the pesto. Slowly add the olive oil and cooled cashews. Use a spatula to scrape down the sides of the bowl between pulsing. Store, covered, in the refrigerator for up to 5 days.

Try serving this salsa over grilled tuna, salmon, swordfish or chicken breast with a side of rice for an incredibly satisfying and refreshing meal. Rub the fish or meat with a little ground coriander, sea salt and freshly ground black pepper before grilling or searing.

PER ¼ CUP

CALORIES: 39.3

FAT: 1.0G

PROTEIN: 2.5G

CARBOHYDRATE: 5.6G

CHOLESTEROL: 0MG

SODIUM: 412MG

MAKES 1¼ CUPS	PREPARATION TIME: 20 MINUTES

1 grapefruit

2 oranges

1 lemon

1 lime

1 teaspoon extra-virgin olive oil

1 tablespoon minced red onion

½ teaspoon minced cilantro

Sea salt

1. With a sharp paring knife, trim the skin of all the citrus. Cut close enough to remove the white pith between the outer skin and the "meat." Cut between the membranes and remove all edible fruit. Carefully pick out the seeds and cut the larger pieces in half.

2. In a glass mixing bowl, gently toss the citrus with the olive oil, onion and cilantro. Season with a pinch of salt.

3. Serve over grilled tuna, salmon, swordfish or chicken breast.

Totally
daiRy-Free
Cooking

✱ MISO WASABI COULIS

Josie's customers usually request this sauce with seafood more than any other sauce on the menu. It takes a little time to make but it's well worth it. It's *powerful*, so you just need a little bit. It is a spicy creamy sauce that's awesome on fish, especially grilled fish, Seared Yellowfin Tuna Burger (page 98) and Three-Grain Vegetable Burger (page 114). This is bound to become a family favorite.

PER 2 TABLESPOONS

CALORIES: 151.8

FAT: 15.2G

PROTEIN: 1.6G

CARBOHYDRATE: 1.6G

CHOLESTEROL: 0MG

SODIUM: 108MG

MAKES 2 CUPS   PREPARATION TIME: 20 MINUTES, PLUS 2 HOURS REFRIGERATION

¼ cup egg whites (from about
   2 eggs)
½ cup canola oil
1 tablespoon red miso
1 tablespoon tamari soy sauce
1 teaspoon fresh lemon juice, or
   Japanese *ponzu* sauce

5 tablespoons rice wine (*mirin*
5 tablespoons rice wine vinegar
¾ cup Japanese *wasabi* mustard
   powder (see Note)
½ cup extra-virgin olive oil

In a small food processor or using an electric handheld blender, blend together the egg whites and canola oil. Add the miso, tamari, lemon juice, wine, vinegar and *wasabi* and combine. While mixing, slowly add the olive oil to form a creamy thick emulsion. Refrigerate at least 2 hours before serving. Store, covered, in the refrigerator for up to 2 weeks.

NOTE: Buy *wasabi* powder in the smallest tin you can find. And store it in a cool dry place. It will stay fresh for 1 to 2 years.

SAUCes

✱ 149

✳ RED MISO–MANGO DIPPING SAUCE

PER ¼ CUP

CALORIES: 65.3

FAT: 1.3G

PROTEIN: 2.6G

CARBOHYDRATE: 8.3G

CHOLESTEROL: 0MG

SODIUM: 755MG

This is a great dipping sauce for dumplings. For a special surprise, try this as a dipping sauce the next time you bring sushi or sashimi home.

MAKES 2½ CUPS   **PREPARATION TIME: 30 MINUTES**

¾ cup red or regular miso

½ cup rice wine (*mirin*)

¼ cup fresh lemon juice (from 1 to 2 lemons), or Japanese *ponzu* sauce

½ cup diced mango

2 tablespoons trimmed and finely sliced scallions

In a mixing bowl, whisk together ¾ cup water, the miso, wine and lemon juice. Add the mango and scallions and refrigerate until ready to use. Store, covered, in the refrigerator for up to 2 weeks.

Totally
daiRY-free
cooking

✳ TOMATO BASIL CONCASSE

This sauce is the epitome of summer-ripe tomatoes and fresh basil. There's nothing like this combination for a fresh-tasting addition to any meal. You can put it over everything from grilled chicken or fish to mesclun greens, or mix it in with cold pasta for a great summer salad. For a variation, use some yellow heirloom tomatoes for a nice multicolored salsa.

PER ¼ CUP

CALORIES: 34.4

FAT: 2G

PROTEIN: 0.7G

CARBOHYDRATE: 3.9G

CHOLESTEROL: 0MG

SODIUM: 125MG

MAKES 2 CUPS   **PREPARATION TIME: 15 MINUTES**

10 ripe plum tomatoes, seeded and diced

6 fresh basil leaves, julienned

2 teaspoons balsamic vinegar

1 tablespoon extra-virgin olive oil

1 tablespoon rice wine (*mirin*)

½ teaspoon sea salt

Freshly ground black pepper

In a mixing bowl, toss all the ingredients together gently. Refrigerate until ready to serve. Store, covered, for up to 2 days in your refrigerator.

SAUces

✳ 151

✳ ROASTED TOMATO VINAIGRETTE

PER ¼ CUP

CALORIES: 103.2

FAT: 7.5G

PROTEIN: 1.8G

CARBOHYDRATE: 9.4G

CHOLESTEROL: 0MG

SODIUM: 64MG

Although this sauce is perfect to serve with the Roasted Eggplant–Wild Mushroom Cakes (page 28), it also goes well on grilled fish and chicken, especially in the summer months when the tomatoes are extra meaty and ripe.

MAKES 2 CUPS   **PREPARATION TIME: 45 MINUTES**

12 ripe plum tomatoes

1 teaspoon minced garlic

1 teaspoon minced shallots

4 tablespoons extra-virgin olive oil

2 tablespoons Dijon mustard

2 tablespoons balsamic vinegar

4 fresh basil leaves, chopped

Sea salt and freshly ground black
    pepper

1. Preheat the oven to 325°F. Cut each tomato in 3 pieces. In a mixing bowl, toss the tomatoes with the garlic, shallots, 1 tablespoon of the olive oil, and the Dijon mustard. Place the mixture in a shallow baking dish and roast for 30 minutes. (In the summer months, put this mixture in an aluminum foil pouch and place on the grill for a smoky flavor. Let cool for 20 minutes.)

2. Transfer the mixture to a food processor and puree. Add the vinegar and basil and mix. Season with salt and pepper to taste. While mixing, slowly drizzle in the remaining 3 tablespoons olive oil to form an emulsified mixture. Refrigerate for up to 3 days.

Totally
dairy-free
Cooking

✳ MANGO, TOMATO AND BLACK BEAN SALSA

This is an extremely quick and easy recipe that's almost fat free yet still exploding with flavor. Add ½ cup of diced ripe avocado for a creamier, richer salsa. You can substitute papaya or pear for the mango to make a seasonal version. This salsa makes a great garnish for the Pan-Seared Black Bean Dumplings (page 34). It keeps refrigerated for up to 3 days.

PER ¼ CUP
CALORIES: 72.3
FAT: 2G
PROTEIN: 2.5G
CARBOHYDRATE: 12.1G
CHOLESTEROL: 0MG
SODIUM: 4MG

MAKES 2 CUPS　　　　　　　　　　　**PREPARATION TIME: 15 MINUTES**

1 medium mango
1 medium red-ripe tomato, seeded
　and diced (about ½ cup)
3 scallions, trimmed and thinly sliced
　(about ¼ cup)
½ jalapeño, seeded
1 cup cooked or canned black beans

Sea salt and freshly ground black
　pepper
1 tablespoon extra-virgin olive oil
1 tablespoon rice wine (*mirin*)
Juice of 1 lime
8 mint leaves, julienned

Peel and slice the mango. Dice the flesh and place in a mixing bowl. Add the tomatoes, scallions and jalapeño, and mix. Gently fold in the black beans and season with salt and pepper to taste. Add the olive oil, wine, lime juice and mint. Toss gently and serve ¼ cup over your favorite grilled or seared fish fillet or chicken breast.

SAUCES

✳ STIR-FRY SAUCE

PER 2 TABLESPOONS

CALORIES: 28.2

FAT: 0.1G

PROTEIN: 0.9G

CARBOHYDRATE: 3.1G

CHOLESTEROL: 0MG

SODIUM: 319MG

This is the kind of sauce you want to have in the refrigerator all the time, especially if you're constantly on the go. It's quick and you can throw anything into a wok or stir-fry pan and make a healthful and delicious meal.

MAKES 2½ CUPS OR TWENTY 2-TABLESPOON SERVINGS   PREPARATION TIME: 20 MINUTES

½ cup cooking sherry or marsala

2 tablespoons minced garlic

2 tablespoons minced shallots

¼ cup grated fresh ginger

½ cup rice wine (*mirin*)

½ cup tamari soy sauce

2 tablespoons arrowroot

1. In a small saucepan over medium-high heat, combine the sherry, garlic, shallots and ginger, and bring to a boil. Reduce the heat and simmer for 5 minutes. Add the wine, tamari and 2 cups of water and return to a boil. Reduce the heat and simmer for 3 minutes.

2. In a small bowl, mix together the arrowroot with 2 tablespoons of water to form a paste. Add to the sauce, stir, and simmer for 2 to 3 minutes more. Remove from the heat. It can be stored, covered, in the refrigerator for up to 2 weeks.

Totally
dairy-free
cooking

✳ TERIYAKI SAUCE

This is an excellent fat-free sauce sure to delight die-hard vegetarians and carnivores alike. It's perfect for a quick glaze on broiled tofu, tempeh, breast of chicken or broiled salmon. It can even be brushed on root vegetables before roasting or added to leafy green vegetables while sautéing or after steaming.

PER 3 TABLESPOONS

CALORIES: 9.7

FAT: 0G

PROTEIN: 0.8G

CARBOHYDRATE: 1.9G

CHOLESTEROL: 0MG

SODIUM: 397MG

MAKES 2¼ CUPS   **PREPARATION TIME: 30 MINUTES**

6 tablespoons tamari soy sauce

6 tablespoons fresh lime juice (from 4 to 6 limes), or Japanese *ponzu* sauce

½ cup fruit juice concentrate, apple or white grape

1½ tablespoons arrowroot

1. In a small saucepan, bring 1¼ cups of water, the tamari and lime juice to a boil. While the sauce is boiling, add the fruit juice concentrate, reduce the heat, and simmer for 3 minutes.

2. In a small bowl, mix together the arrowroot with 2 tablespoons of water. Add this to the simmering sauce and cook, stirring, for 2 minutes. Remove from the heat, cool and store in an airtight container in the refrigerator for up to 2 weeks.

SAUces

✳ 155

Condiments are the backbone of your kitchen. Everybody uses them, but people take them for granted. If you use condiments a lot, then you might want to make some of them yourself just to experience what's in your favorites. Sometimes, the difference between a good and a great meal depends on the condiments used with it. Shouldn't a home-cooked meal be accented with a home-cooked condiment?

I know what you're thinking—it would be easier simply to buy these products, but that wouldn't be as much fun! All of these recipes are dairy-free, lowfat and healthful versions of the store-bought equivalents. Try using them as spreads on leftovers to create a new flavor out of yesterday's dinner. The salsas, Guacamole (page 161) and Black Bean Hummus (page 160) also can be used as a whole appetizer plate in themselves, served with baked tortilla chips or pita crisps.

✳ BLACK BEAN HUMMUS

PER ¼ CUP

CALORIES: 199.2

FAT: 2.6G

PROTEIN: 11.8G

CARBOHYDRATE: 33.8G

CHOLESTEROL: 0MG

SODIUM: 256MG

Hummus has become pretty mainstream these days, and there's nothing better than homemade hummus. The flavor is so rich and delicious. No store-bought brand could stand against this hearty version. For variety, replace the black beans with white beans, chickpeas or even soybeans. Serve with rice crackers, pita crisps or Belgian endive. Try adding a tablespoon of finely chopped dill, chervil and/or basil to the finished hummus for an herbal flavor. Try substituting black soybeans for the regular black beans for a nuttier flavor.

MAKES 1 CUP	PREPARATION TIME: 5 MINUTES

1 cup cooked or canned black beans

2 teaspoons minced garlic

1 tablespoon freshly squeezed
    lemon juice

1 tablespoon tamari soy sauce

1 tablespoon tahini (sesame paste)

1 teaspoon honey

2 dashes Tabasco sauce

Salt and freshly ground black pepper

Add all the ingredients to a food processor. Blend on low speed until roughly chopped, then increase to high speed to get a smooth consistency. Season with salt and pepper to taste. Store, covered, in the refrigerator for up to 7 days.

NOTES: Reserve some of the cooking liquid from the black beans and add it to the processor if necessary. This will give you a smoother texture and keep the ingredients from binding up. If you are using canned black beans, the canning liquid will give you the desired results.

Totally dairy-free cooking

✳ GUACAMOLE

Some guacamole recipes call for sour cream to give it a rich creamy taste and texture, but not mine. Use ripe black-skinned Hass avocados when preparing this dish. They are creamier and have less water content than other kinds of avocados and that will replace the need for sour cream. Lemon juice will keep the avocado from discoloring. Keeping the pit in the finished guacamole will also help keep the freshness and flavor until serving time. A stainless steel or metal bowl may cause the avocado to discolor. Serve within twenty-four hours.

PER ¼ CUP

CALORIES: 87.9

FAT: 7.8G

PROTEIN: 1.3G

CARBOHYDRATE: 5.3G

CHOLESTEROL: 0MG

SODIUM: 8MG

MAKES 2 CUPS   **PREPARATION TIME: 15 MINUTES**

2 ripe Hass avocados
1 teaspoon freshly squeezed lemon
   juice
½ cup finely chopped red onions
½ cup seeded and diced plum
   tomatoes

1 tablespoon finely chopped fresh
   cilantro
½ teaspoon Tabasco sauce
Salt and freshly ground black pepper

1. Slice the avocados in half and remove the pit. Remove the skin and chop into medium dice. Place in a plastic or glass mixing bowl, immediately add the lemon juice and gently toss.

2. Add the onions, tomatoes, cilantro and Tabasco to the bowl and mix with a fork. Season with salt and pepper to taste.

CONdimenTS

✳ 161

✳ TAHINI SAUCE

PER 2 TABLESPOONS

CALORIES: 104.4

FAT: 7.6G

PROTEIN: 3G

CARBOHYDRATE: 7.8G

CHOLESTEROL: 0MG

SODIUM: 128MG

This smooth sesame-flavored sauce will impress your vegetarian friends who are used to the store-bought versions. It's as good as it gets. Try it on vegetable burgers, wrap sandwiches and in Black Bean Hummus (page 160).

MAKES 2 CUPS	PREPARATION TIME: 15 MINUTES

1 cup tahini (sesame paste)

2 tablespoons tamari soy sauce

⅓ cup rice wine vinegar

1 teaspoon fresh lemon juice

½ teaspoon minced garlic

1 teaspoon ground coriander

¼ teaspoon ground cumin

3 tablespoons fruit juice concentrate, apple or white grape

In a large bowl or container, using an electric handheld or regular blender, puree all the ingredients together with ½ cup of water. Store, covered, in the refrigerator for up to 7 days.

Totally
dairy-free
cooking

✳ TOFU SOUR CREAM

This is great with spicy dishes to take some of the heat off. Use this recipe anytime you desire the taste or texture of real sour cream.

PER 3 TABLESPOONS

CALORIES: 23.2

FAT: 1.3G

PROTEIN: 2.3G

CARBOHYDRATE: 1.2G

CHOLESTEROL: 0MG

SODIUM: 318MG

MAKES 2¼ CUPS   **PREPARATION TIME: 10 MINUTES**

10 ounces soft tofu

4 tablespoons freshly squeezed
   lemon juice (from about 2 lemons)

2 teaspoons sea salt

¼ cup minced fresh cilantro

6 tablespoons plain soy milk

Puree all the ingredients in a food processor until smooth. Chill and serve. Keep the leftovers refrigerated in an airtight container for up to 7 days.

CONdiments

✳ APPLE CRANBERRY CHUTNEY

Take some of the tartness out of your traditional cranberry sauce by using apples, as in this chutney. Serve it with Thanksgiving Turkey (page 135). It's also a great spread on chicken, turkey or grilled tuna wrap sandwiches. For a vegetarian switch, try it on roasted butternut squash, or in a wrap sandwich with Seared Asian Tofu (page 184).

MAKES 2 CUPS   **PREPARATION TIME: 30 MINUTES**

2 large Granny Smith apples
¾ cup orange juice
¼ cup port wine
¼ cup cider vinegar
½ cup fresh or frozen (thawed) cranberries

¼ cup maple syrup
Salt, ground cinnamon and nutmeg, optional

When freezing condiments or any other food item, squeeze all of the air out of the freezer bag before you seal it and put it into the freezer. This will prevent ice crystals from forming on the food and better preserve the flavor and texture of the item.

1. Peel and core the apples and cut them into medium dice.

2. In a medium saucepan, bring the orange juice, port and vinegar to a boil. Add the apples and cranberries, bring back to a boil, reduce the heat, and simmer for 15 to 20 minutes. Add the maple syrup, stir and remove from the heat.

3. Roughly puree the mixture in a food processor or with an electric handheld blender. Season with a pinch of salt, cinnamon and nutmeg, if desired. Store, covered, in the refrigerator for up to 1 week.

Totally dairy-free Cooking

✳ BASIC KETCHUP

Start your kids on this ketchup early and they'll never want the store-bought sugar-laden version again. You can zip up this ketchup by adding 1 to 2 tablespoons of pureed chipotle peppers or 4 to 5 pureed roasted cloves of garlic just before pureeing the ketchup. Try adding a pinch of ground coriander or ground cumin with hot sauce for another terrific taste.

PER 2 TABLESPOONS

CALORIES: 26.1

FAT: 0.8G

PROTEIN: 0.5G

CARBOHYDRATE: 5G

CHOLESTEROL: 0MG

SODIUM: 111MG

MAKES 2½ CUPS　　　　　　　**PREPARATION TIME: 1 HOUR**

1 tablespoon olive oil

1 teaspoon minced garlic

1 cup chopped onions

¼ cup rice wine vinegar

¼ cup cider vinegar

12 canned whole plum tomatoes,
　　chopped

1 teaspoon sea salt

2 tablespoons fruit juice concentrate,
　　apple or white grape, or maple
　　syrup

2 tablespoons tomato paste, optional

1. In a medium saucepan over medium heat, heat the olive oil. Add the garlic and onions and cook, stirring, until the onions are translucent, about 3 minutes. Add both vinegars and stir. Add the tomatoes and salt and stir. Let simmer for 15 to 20 minutes.

2. Remove the pan from the heat and let cool slightly. With an electric handheld blender, or in a food processor or blender, puree the sauce. Add the fruit juice concentrate (and tomato paste, if desired) and blend again. Refrigerate, covered, for up to 2 weeks.

CONDIMENTS

✳ ANCHO CHILI DRY RUB

PER TEASPOON

CALORIES: 8.5

FAT: 0.2G

PROTEIN: 0.2G

CARBOHYDRATE: 1.4G

CHOLESTEROL: 0MG

SODIUM: 326MG

This rub is great for poultry, fish and all types of burgers if you're looking for a delectable Southwestern flavor. For added zest, rub it on the meats up to twenty-four hours in advance and place in the refrigerator. Drizzle a little bit of olive oil on the surface of the meat to help evenly distribute the rub.

MAKES 3 TABLESPOONS   **PREPARATION TIME: 5 MINUTES**

1 tablespoon ancho chili powder   1½ teaspoons sea salt

1 tablespoon dried oregano   1½ teaspoons sucanat sugar

In a coffee grinder or food processor, grind all the ingredients together and store in an airtight container. This will keep for months in a dry cool place.

Totally
dairy-free
cooking

166 ✳

✳ JOSIE'S BARBECUE SAUCE

You can brush this on everything from tofu to spare ribs. This lightly spiced all-purpose barbecue sauce will appeal to everyone. For a little more spice, add hot sauce or chili peppers to taste.

MAKES 2¼ CUPS　　　　　　　　　　**PREPARATION TIME: 45 MINUTES**

1 tablespoon extra-virgin olive oil

½ teaspoon minced shallots

1 teaspoon minced garlic

½ tablespoon minced fresh ginger

1 cup chopped onions

4 fresh basil leaves

½ cup cider vinegar

2 tablespoons tomato paste

10 whole canned plum tomatoes (14½-ounce can)

1 tablespoon minced fresh cilantro

1½ teaspoons chili powder

1 teaspoon ground coriander

½ teaspoon ground cumin

1 teaspoon sea salt

⅛ teaspoon freshly ground black pepper

1 tablespoon fruit juice concentrate, apple or white grape, or maple syrup

Make sure when you are storing condiments in your refrigerator that you date them. This way you take out the guesswork.

1. Heat a medium saucepan over medium heat and add the olive oil. Add the shallots, garlic, ginger, onions and basil, and cook, stirring, until the onions and shallots are golden, about 5 minutes.

2. Add the vinegar, tomato paste, tomatoes, cilantro, chili powder, coriander, cumin, salt, pepper and fruit juice concentrate. Simmer over low heat for 20 minutes. Cool slightly and puree with an electric handheld blender or food processor. Store, covered, in the refrigerator for up to 2 weeks.

CondimenTs

* ANCHO CHILI AND SUN-DRIED CHERRY BARBECUE SAUCE

PER ¼ CUP

CALORIES: 82

FAT: 1G

PROTEIN: 0.7G

CARBOHYDRATE: 20G

CHOLESTEROL: 0MG

SODIUM: 358MG

Impress your friends by offering two very different and delicious barbecue sauces at your next party. This makes a great alternative sauce, with a totally different flavor than most barbecue sauces. This flavoring is great with grilled poultry or meats. It's also a good dipping sauce with most tortilla wraps.

MAKES 4 CUPS | **PREPARATION TIME: 45 SERVINGS**

1 cup rice wine vinegar

1 cup cider vinegar

¼ teaspoon ground cloves

¼ teaspoon ground allspice

¼ teaspoon ground coriander

1 tablespoon extra-virgin olive oil

½ cup chopped onions

2 teaspoons minced garlic

2 cups Basic Ketchup (page 165)

½ cup sucanat sugar

2 tablespoons molasses, or barley malt

2 tablespoons ancho chili powder

1½ cups sun-dried cherries

Sea salt and freshly ground black pepper

1. In a medium saucepan, bring both vinegars to a boil. Add the cloves, allspice and coriander. Reduce the heat and simmer until the liquid is reduced by half, about 10 minutes.

2. In a nonstick skillet, heat the olive oil over medium heat. Add the onions and garlic and cook, stirring, until the onions are translucent, about 3 minutes. Add the ketchup, sugar, molasses, 2 cups of water, the chili powder and cherries. Transfer into the saucepan with the vinegars and bring to a boil. Reduce the heat and simmer for 25 to 30 minutes. Puree with an electric handheld blender or food processor. Season with salt and pepper to taste. Refrigerate, covered, until ready to use, or up to 2 weeks.

Totally
dairy-free
cooking

✳ ROASTED CORN–CHIPOTLE SALSA

Warning! Once you dip your first chip in this salsa, you won't be able to stop. You can spice up everything from chili and soups to fajitas and burritos with this taste of the Southwest. This is excellent on meat loaf or with your favorite Mexican food. No store-bought salsa can touch the flavors in this. This is a salsa aficionado's dream, with flavor, depth and consistency.

MAKES 2 CUPS   PREPARATION TIME: 40 MINUTES, PLUS SEVERAL HOURS REFRIGERATION

1 tablespoon olive oil

1 teaspoon minced garlic

½ cup minced onions

1 cup fresh or frozen corn kernels

½ cup cider vinegar

One 14½-ounce can diced tomatoes

1 teaspoon honey

1 tablespoon chopped canned chipotle peppers (with canning sauce)

2 teaspoons tomato paste

1 teaspoon sea salt

2 tablespoons medium chopped fresh cilantro

1. In a nonstick skillet over medium heat, heat the olive oil. Add the garlic and cook, stirring, until golden, 1 minute. Reduce the heat to medium-low, add the onions and corn, and cook, stirring, until the corn browns, about 15 minutes.

2. Transfer the contents of the skillet to a small saucepan and add the vinegar. Cook until the liquid is reduced by half, about 5 minutes. Add the tomatoes and simmer for 8 minutes. Add the honey, chipotle peppers, tomato paste, salt and cilantro. Simmer 3 more minutes and remove from the heat.

3. Transfer into a storage container and chill several hours before serving. Refrigerate for up to 7 days.

CoNdimeNTs

✳ THREE-PEPPER SALSA

PER ¼ CUP

CALORIES: 33.6

FAT: 1.9G

PROTEIN: 0.7G

CARBOHYDRATE: 4.6G

CHOLESTEROL: 0MG

SODIUM: 242MG

Finally, a place to use all those leftover pepper scraps! Save everything, even the ends, chop them up and use them in this salsa. Add 1 cup of your favorite cooked beans for a heartier condiment. Serve with Guacamole (page 161) and chips, Chicken Fajitas with Cilantro-Walnut Pesto (page 171), Chicken, Brown Rice and Black Bean Burrito (page 124), or the Lump Crab Cakes (page 32).

MAKES 2 CUPS   PREPARATION TIME: 40 MINUTES, PLUS SEVERAL HOURS REFRIGERATION

1 tablespoon olive oil

1 teaspoon minced garlic

½ cup medium chopped yellow onions

1 cup medium chopped bell peppers

1 medium jalapeño, seeded and fine diced

1 teaspoon chili powder

½ cup cider vinegar

One 14½-ounce can diced tomatoes

1 teaspoon sea salt

Freshly ground black pepper

1 tablespoon chopped fresh cilantro

1. In a small saucepan, heat the olive oil over medium heat. Add the garlic and cook, stirring, until golden, 1 minute. Reduce the heat to medium-low, add the onions and bell peppers and cook, stirring, for 10 minutes. Add the jalapeño, chili powder and vinegar. Cook until the liquid is reduced by half, about 5 minutes.

2. Add the tomatoes and simmer for 10 to 12 minutes. Season with the sea salt, black pepper to taste, and the cilantro. Refrigerate for several hours before serving. Store, covered, in the refrigerator for up to 7 days.

Totally
dairy-free
Cooking

✳ CILANTRO-WALNUT PESTO

This is great mixed with any hot pasta or thrown right into your favorite pasta sauce. Try spreading it on a wrap sandwich or inside a fajita. If you can't find the chili garlic paste, you can replace it with one teaspoon of regular chili paste.

PER 1½ TABLESPOONS
CALORIES: 81.1
FAT: 6.9G
PROTEIN: 3G
CARBOHYDRATE: 3.5G
CHOLESTEROL: 0MG
SODIUM: 255MG

MAKES ALMOST 2 CUPS   **PREPARATION TIME: 5 MINUTES**

½ cup packed cilantro leaves
½ cup packed basil leaves
½ cup walnut pieces, lightly toasted
   in a 350°F oven for 5 minutes
¼ cup balsamic vinegar
1 teaspoon minced garlic
1¼ teaspoons sea salt

1 teaspoon chili garlic paste, or Thai
   chili paste
2 teaspoons honey
1 teaspoon freshly squeezed lemon
   juice
1 teaspoon extra-virgin olive oil
Freshly ground black pepper

Place all the ingredients into a food processor with ¼ cup water and puree until smooth. Store, covered, in the refrigerator for up to 5 days.

condiments

✳ 171

✳ PUMPKIN SEED, BASIL AND MISO PESTO

PER 2 TABLESPOONS

CALORIES: 36.7

FAT: 2.2G

PROTEIN: 1.4G

CARBOHYDRATE: 3.7G

CHOLESTEROL: 0MG

SODIUM: 54MG

This versatile pesto can be served as a spread for sandwiches, dolloped on pasta or swirled in the Roasted Kabocha Squash Soup (page 47) for extra flavor. Try it on top of your favorite seasonal sautéed vegetables.

MAKES 1¼ CUPS   **PREPARATION TIME: 15 MINUTES**

2 cups tightly packed basil leaves

2 cloves garlic

2 tablespoons shelled pumpkin seeds

2 teaspoons fresh lemon juice

2 teaspoons chickpea miso, or
     regular miso

1 teaspoon honey

1 tablespoon extra-virgin olive oil

1. Preheat the oven to 325°F. Toast the pumpkin seeds for 5 minutes.

2. Place all ingredients in a food processor with 2 tablespoons water and blend until smooth. Store, covered, in the refrigerator for up to 5 days.

Totally
dairy-free
Cooking

✳ SWEET POTATO, CARROT AND ONION DIPPING SAUCE

This was the first bread dipping sauce I ever served at Josie's. Our customers can't get enough of this stuff. In fact, they often tell us to take it away from the table so they can still have room for their dinner. Serve with your favorite bread, tortillas or crackers as a snack. This sauce is also great as a spread on your favorite wrap sandwich.

PER ¼ CUP

CALORIES: 63

FAT: 0.9G

PROTEIN: 1.2G

CARBOHYDRATE: 12.9G

CHOLESTEROL: 0MG

SODIUM: 104MG

MAKES 2½ CUPS   **PREPARATION TIME: 1 HOUR AND 10 MINUTES**

1 pound sweet potatoes, scrubbed

1 medium carrot, peeled and thinly sliced

½ medium onion, peeled and thinly sliced

1 tablespoon tahini (sesame paste)

½ teaspoon sea salt

½ teaspoon curry powder

¼ teaspoon ground cumin

1. Preheat the oven to 400°F. Wrap the sweet potatoes in foil and roast for 50 minutes or until cooked through. Uncover and let sit for 10 minutes. Remove the skin and chop the potatoes into medium-size pieces.

2. In a small saucepan, bring 1 cup of water to a boil. Add the carrot and onion, return to a boil, reduce the heat and simmer for 10 minutes. Do not drain; set aside.

3. In a food processor, combine the sweet potato, the carrot-onion mixture with the cooking liquid, and the remaining ingredients. Puree until smooth. Refrigerate, covered, until ready to serve or for up to 3 days.

Have plenty of stackable lidded plastic containers on hand to store your condiments in the refrigerator. If you keep them orderly, they won't get lost in the back.

CONdimeNTs

✳ 173

✳ SUN-DRIED TOMATO DIPPING SAUCE

PER 3 TABLESPOONS

CALORIES: 66.3

FAT: 2G

PROTEIN: 3.3G

CARBOHYDRATE: 10.1G

CHOLESTEROL: 0MG

SODIUM: 159MG

It's like butter (except, of course, there's absolutely no dairy in this recipe . . .). If you're going to make this sauce, make sure you have plenty of bread around because it's addictive. It has great flavor and you'll never want buttered bread again.

MAKES 1½ CUPS   **PREPARATION TIME: 10 MINUTES**

1 cup sun-dried tomatoes (dry, not oil-packed)

1 cup canned or cooked white beans

1 tablespoon balsamic vinegar

1 tablespoon extra-virgin olive oil

½ teaspoon minced garlic

1 tablespoon tomato paste

5 fresh basil leaves

Sea salt and freshly ground black pepper

1. In a small saucepan, bring 1 quart of water to a boil. Add the tomatoes and blanch for 90 seconds. Drain, reserving ¾ cup of the cooking water, and set aside.

2. In a food processor, puree the tomatoes with ½ cup water and all remaining ingredients to a smooth consistency. Add extra water for a lighter consistency. Store, covered, in the refrigerator for up to 5 days.

Totally
dairy-free
cooking

Mashed potatoes without milk and butter? Impossible, right? Not anymore! These side dishes are guaranteed to perk up any meal and you're absolutely going to love how easy they are to make. In fact, they're so good, you can easily combine a few of these and make a complete meal. These are some of the most famous and favorite recipes from my restaurant, Josie's, and now you can try them at home.

✳ SOY CREAMED SPINACH

CALORIES: 92.8

FAT: 4.3G

PROTEIN: 8.1G

CARBOHYDRATE: 8G

CHOLESTEROL: 0MG

SODIUM: 245MG

My version of this classic creamed spinach tastes better than any one of those fat- and dairy-laden steakhouse recipes. My secret is the Pernod, which gives it a special licorice-like flavor. Pernod can be purchased at any liquor store.

MAKES 6 SERVINGS   PREPARATION TIME: 30 MINUTES

3 cups frozen chopped spinach (approximately 1½ 10-ounce packages)
1 tablespoon soy margarine
¼ cup chopped onions
2 teaspoons minced shallots
2 teaspoons minced garlic

2 tablespoons Pernod
1½ cups plain soy milk
1½ teaspoons arrowroot
Sea salt and freshly ground black pepper
¼ cup soy Parmesan

1. Defrost the spinach in a colander. Press out the excess moisture.

2. In a medium saucepan over medium heat, heat the margarine. Add the onions, shallots and garlic and cook, stirring, until the onions are translucent, 3 to 4 minutes. Add the Pernod to deglaze the pan, and stir. Add the spinach, reduce the heat to medium-low, and cook, stirring, for 5 minutes.

3. Meanwhile, in a small saucepan, bring the soy milk to a simmer. In a small bowl, mix the arrowroot with 2 teaspoons of water, add the mixture to the simmering soy milk, and stir.

4. Add the soy milk to the spinach and mix thoroughly. Season with the salt and black pepper to taste. Mix in the Parmesan, remove from the stove top, and serve.

Totally dairy-free cooking

✳ TOMATO AND SOY MOZZARELLA POLENTA

Polenta is really wonderful as a side dish with almost anything you serve. You can also spread the polenta evenly in a shallow pan, cut it into squares, diamonds or circles and bake in a 350°F oven or on a grill for 30 minutes or until crisp. Try this polenta as a filler for a dairy-free, meatless soy lasagne, alternating layers with Vodka Tomato Soy "Cream" Sauce (page 78) and soy mozzarella. Try the rice lasagne noodles from De Boles for a wheat-free alternative.

CALORIES: 109.2

FAT: 2.6G

PROTEIN: 6G

CARBOHYDRATE: 16.2G

CHOLESTEROL: 0MG

SODIUM: 218MG

MAKES 8 SERVINGS	PREPARATION TIME: 40 MINUTES

1½ cups plain soy milk

1 cup yellow quick-cooking fine
   cornmeal

½ cup tomato sauce
   (page 74)

2 tablespoons soy Parmesan

¼ cup grated soy mozzarella

In a small, heavy-duty saucepan, bring the soy milk and 1½ cups of water to a boil. Add the cornmeal and mix well with a whisk. Reduce the heat to medium-low and cook, stirring frequently to avoid burning, for 10 minutes. Add the tomato sauce and mix well. Mix in the soy Parmesan and soy mozzarella just before serving.

On the Side

✳ THREE-POTATO MASH

CALORIES: 133.2

FAT: 3.7G

PROTEIN: 4.1G

CARBOHYDRATE: 22.6G

CHOLESTEROL: 0MG

SODIUM: 17MG

A variety of potatoes gives this mash a unique combination of flavors and textures you simply can't get from using just one type. You don't need to add milk and butter to get a rich creamy taste. Keep the skin on the potatoes to preserve all of the nutrients.

MAKES 10 TO 12 SERVINGS	PREPARATION TIME: 50 MINUTES

1 pound Yukon Gold potatoes
1 pound Idaho potatoes
1 pound red potatoes
1 cup lowfat, plain soy milk
1 medium shallot, chopped
2 teaspoons minced garlic
1 tablespoon freshly grated
   horseradish, optional

Sea salt and freshly ground black
   pepper
2 tablespoons extra-virgin olive oil
¼ cup minced fresh parsley
10 fresh tarragon leaves, chopped
2 fresh sage leaves, chopped

Most side dishes can be reheated the next day with a little extra liquid. For example, add a little extra soy milk to any of the potatoes while heating.

1. Scrub and quarter all the potatoes, but do not peel. Place in a medium saucepan and cover with water. Bring to a boil and reduce the heat and simmer for about 40 minutes, or until the potatoes are cooked through.

2. Meanwhile, in a small saucepan, heat the soy milk. Do not boil. Add the shallot, garlic, and horseradish, if desired. Season with salt and pepper to taste. Set aside.

3. In a colander, drain the potatoes thoroughly and place them in a mixing bowl. Add the soy milk mixture and mash well with a heavy-duty wire whip. Drizzle in the olive oil, add the fresh herbs and season with salt and pepper. Serve warm with anything.

Totally
dairy-free
cooking

✳ MASHED SWEET POTATOES

Sweet potatoes aren't just good at Thanksgiving. This delicious mash is a treat all year long! Try it with not so obvious meals such as duck or chicken. Orange juice, soy milk and maple syrup more than make up for the butter and cream usually used in mashed potatoes.

CALORIES: 98.3

FAT: 0.7G

PROTEIN: 1.9G

CARBOHYDRATE: 22G

CHOLESTEROL: 0MG

SODIUM: 11MG

MAKES 6 SERVINGS   **PREPARATION TIME: 2 HOURS**

3 medium sweet potatoes (3 pounds), scrubbed

½ cup lowfat, vanilla soy milk

¼ cup sun-dried cranberries

¼ cup fresh orange juice (from about 1 orange)

¼ teaspoon ground cinnamon

¼ teaspoon ground nutmeg

Sea salt and freshly ground black pepper

1 tablespoon maple syrup

1. Preheat the oven to 375°F. Roast the sweet potatoes on a baking sheet for 1½ hours. Turn the sweet potatoes once to ensure even cooking.

2. Meanwhile, in a small saucepan, heat the soy milk, but do not boil. Add the cranberries, orange juice, cinnamon, nutmeg, and salt and black pepper to taste. Set aside.

3. When the sweet potatoes are done, remove from the oven and let them cool for 15 minutes. When cool enough to handle, remove the skin. Pass the sweet potatoes through a food mill or mash in a bowl with a heavy-duty wire whip. Be patient! The end result is worth the effort.

4. In a bowl, combine the soy milk mixture with the sweet potatoes and mix with a large spoon. Season with salt and pepper. Add the maple syrup and serve warm.

On the Side

CALORIES: 102.3

FAT: 3G

PROTEIN: 2G

CARBOHYDRATE: 17G

CHOLESTEROL: 0MG

SODIUM: 91MG

This dish goes well with any of the recipes that contain miso. Or, try it with one of the meatloafs for a good old-fashioned home-cooked meal with an Asian twist. For a smoother consistency, use a food processor or food mill to mash the potatoes.

MAKES 4 SERVINGS   **PREPARATION TIME: 1 HOUR**

1 pound Idaho potatoes

2 teaspoons *wasabi* powder (or to taste)

1½ tablespoons lowfat, plain soy milk

1 tablespoon soy margarine

1 tablespoon trimmed and thinly sliced scallions

Sea salt and freshly ground black pepper

1. Peel and dice the potatoes. Place in a small saucepan and cover with water. Bring to a boil and cook for 15 to 20 minutes, or until soft.

2. Drain the potatoes in a colander. In a mixing bowl, combine the potatoes with the remaining ingredients and mash with a heavy-duty wire whisk. Serve warm.

Totally
daiRY-Free
cookiNg

✳ ROOT VEGETABLE PUREE

Root vegetables are becoming very popular in restaurants. This puree is a surprising switch from mashed potatoes. The combination gives this dish a unique taste that is hearty and satisfying. For a spicier puree, add some freshly grated ginger. For a smoother consistency, use a food processor or food mill.

CALORIES: 88.3

FAT: 3.7G

PROTEIN: 1.4G

CARBOHYDRATE: 13.3G

CHOLESTEROL: 0MG

SODIUM: 54MG

MAKES 4 SERVINGS	PREPARATION TIME: 1 HOUR

1 medium parsnip

1 medium celery root

1 medium turnip

½ medium sweet potato

1 tablespoon extra-virgin olive oil

2 tablespoons plain soy milk

Sea salt and freshly ground black pepper

1. Peel and cut all the root vegetables into large dice. In a saucepan, bring 2 quarts of water to a boil. Add the vegetables and cook for 15 to 20 minutes or until cooked all the way through.

2. Drain the vegetables in a colander and transfer to a mixing bowl. Mash them with a heavy-duty wire whisk and drizzle in the olive oil and soy milk. Season with salt and pepper to taste.

On the Side

✳ SEARED ASIAN TOFU

CALORIES: 182.2

FAT: 11G

PROTEIN: 18.4G

CARBOHYDRATE: 5.3G

CHOLESTEROL: 0MG

SODIUM: 267MG

This recipe has satisfied my customers at Josie's since the first day we opened our doors. If you've never tried tofu before, I think you'll be surprised at how incredible this tastes. Add this to anything from burritos to stir-fry or as a substitute for meat.

MAKES 4 SERVINGS	PREPARATION TIME: 1 HOUR

1 pound firm tofu

1 tablespoon tamari soy sauce

1 tablespoon rice wine (*mirin*)

1 tablespoon Thai chili-garlic paste

½ teaspoon sesame oil

1 teaspoon extra-virgin olive oil

Freshly ground black pepper

1. Place the tofu on a paper towel on a plate. Set another plate over the tofu and top with a heavy object to remove excess moisture, for about 30 minutes. Slice the tofu lengthwise in 4 equal slices. Place in a shallow Pyrex dish.

2. In a mixing bowl, whisk together all the remaining ingredients. Pour over the tofu. Marinate the tofu for 15 minutes, turning several times to coat.

3. In a nonstick skillet over medium heat, sear the tofu slices for 2 to 3 minutes on each side, or until browned.

Totally
dairy-free
cooking

✳ STEAMED BROCCOLI IN BASIL, WHITE WINE AND GARLIC BROTH

The flavor of broccoli with fresh basil is incredible, and the white wine and garlic combination is not overpowering. This is a great side dish for roasted or grilled meats and seafood. Try some spaghetti or linguine with this dish for a simple but extremely flavorful vegetarian meal. Garnish with soy Parmesan and fresh basil.

CALORIES: 66

FAT: 3.6G

PROTEIN: 1.4G

CARBOHYDRATE: 3.3G

CHOLESTEROL: 0MG

SODIUM: 9MG

MAKES 4 SERVINGS   **PREPARATION TIME: 30 MINUTES**

1 bunch broccoli (approximately
   1½ pounds)
1 tablespoon olive oil
4 cloves garlic, halved
½ cup packed fresh basil leaves

½ cup white wine
Sea salt and freshly ground black
   pepper
¼ teaspoon red pepper flakes,
   optional

For a nice switch on presentation, try serving your side dishes on a separate plate rather than on the same plate with the entrée.

1. Clean and trim the broccoli. Cut off the large stems, peel and slice. Set the sliced stems aside. Chop the florets in half lengthwise and keep in large clusters.

2. In a shallow saucepan with a lid, heat the olive oil over medium-low heat. Add the garlic and cook, stirring, until golden, about 1 minute. Add the sliced broccoli stems and cook for 5 minutes. Add the basil and wine, and simmer for 2 minutes. Add the broccoli florets, season with salt and black pepper to taste, and add the red pepper flakes, if desired. Add ¼ cup of water, cover, steam for 6 to 8 minutes, and serve.

On the
Side

✳ SWEET MISO-GLAZED EGGPLANT

CALORIES: 81.2
FAT: 1.7G
PROTEIN: 2.9G
CARBOHYDRATE: 15G
CHOLESTEROL: 0MG
SODIUM: 665MG

The natural bitterness of the eggplant is the perfect complement to the exotic, sweet taste of the miso. Japanese eggplant is longer and thinner than regular eggplant; it has fewer seeds and less acid. It's great as an appetizer, especially if you're eating sushi.

MAKES 4 SERVINGS	PREPARATION TIME: 1 HOUR

2 whole Japanese eggplant

1 teaspoon sea salt

2 teaspoons chickpea miso, or regular miso

1 tablespoon rice wine (*mirin*)

1 teaspoon tamari soy sauce

1 teaspoon extra-virgin olive oil

1. Slice the eggplant down the middle lengthwise and score on the skin side with shallow X-shaped incisions. Salt the flesh and let it sit for 30 minutes. Rinse well to get all the bitter acid and salt out. Squeeze with paper towels to dry.

2. Preheat the oven to 375°F. In a small mixing bowl, mix together the miso, rice wine and tamari. Set aside.

3. Rub the flesh part of the eggplant with the olive oil and place on a nonstick baking tray. Bake for 20 to 25 minutes or until soft. Remove from the oven.

4. Spread the miso mixture into the eggplant flesh, getting it into the X-shaped incisions. Place in the oven for an additional 10 minutes.

Totally dairy-free cooking

✳ TAMARI BROWN RICE

This high-flavored, lowfat rice goes well with every imaginable stir-fry and teriyaki dish. Try serving leftovers the next day, steamed with Tahini Sauce (page 162) drizzled over it.

CALORIES: 187.7
FAT: 1.3G
PROTEIN: 4.6G
CARBOHYDRATE: 37.2G
CHOLESTEROL: 0MG
SODIUM: 508MG

MAKES 16 SERVINGS   **PREPARATION TIME: 45 MINUTES**

4 cups brown rice, washed and dried   ½ cup rice wine (*mirin*)

1 teaspoon minced garlic   ½ cup tamari soy sauce

1 teaspoon chopped fresh ginger

1. Place the rice and 6 cups of water in a medium stockpot and bring to a boil. Boil uncovered for 15 minutes, then reduce the heat to medium and simmer uncovered for another 15 minutes. Remove from the stove and cover the pot for 10 minutes.

2. Add the garlic, ginger, wine, and tamari to the rice. Mix thoroughly and cover an additional 5 minutes before serving.

On the Side

✳ MANGO-SCALLION STICKY RICE

CALORIES: 175.2

FAT: 0.4G

PROTEIN: 3.4G

CARBOHYDRATE: 37.8G

CHOLESTEROL: 0MG

SODIUM: 24MG

This is a white rice that hasn't had the starch washed off, which is what makes it sticky. It is also called sticky rice. It's great with a stir-fry and goes well with miso sauces.

MAKES 4 SERVINGS   **PREPARATION TIME: 45 MINUTES**

2¼ cups water (water and bouillon can be replaced with 2¼ cups of Vegetable Stock, page 45)

2 teaspoons vegetarian bouillon (2 cubes)

2 teaspoons rice wine (*mirin*)

2 teaspoons rice vinegar

1 cup sticky rice (*nishiki*)

2 tablespoons trimmed and thinly sliced scallions

½ cup finely diced mangoes

Sea salt and freshly ground black pepper

In a saucepan with a cover, bring the water to a boil. Add the bouillon, wine and vinegar, then add the rice and bring to a simmer. Reduce the heat and simmer uncovered for 5 to 7 minutes. Stir often to keep rice from sticking to the bottom of the pot. Turn off the heat, cover, and let sit for 20 to 25 minutes, or until rice is cooked through. Mix in the scallions and mangoes and fluff with a fork before serving. Season with salt and pepper as desired.

Totally
dairy-free
cooking

✳ SLOW-COOKED STRING BEANS

The slow cooking time allows the eclectic combination of ingredients really to sink in. This is the kind of dish that tastes even better the next day.

CALORIES: 78.5
FAT: 1.9G
PROTEIN: 2.5G
CARBOHYDRATE: 12G
CHOLESTEROL: 0MG
SODIUM: 35MG

MAKES 8 SERVINGS   **PREPARATION TIME: 1½ HOURS**

1 tablespoon olive oil

½ cup minced shallots

2 pounds string beans, cleaned and
   trimmed

¼ cup dry cooking sherry

¼ cup dry white wine

1 tablespoon balsamic vinegar

1 tablespoon Worcestershire sauce

Sea salt and freshly ground black
   pepper

1 red bell pepper, julienned

1 teaspoon pure maple syrup

½ teaspoon hot sauce, optional

1. In a heavy-duty saucepan over medium heat, heat the olive oil. Add the shallots and cook, stirring, until golden, 2 to 3 minutes. Add the string beans, sherry, wine, vinegar and Worcestershire. Sprinkle with salt and black pepper, cover and reduce to a low simmer. Cook approximately 1 hour, stirring every 20 minutes. Add ¼ cup water if necessary.

2. Add the bell pepper and cook an additional 15 minutes, covered. Remove from the stovetop, and add the maple syrup and hot sauce, if desired. Season again with salt and black pepper before serving.

On the Side

✳ BARBECUE BAKED BEANS

CALORIES: 105

FAT: 2.7G

PROTEIN: 5.6G

CARBOHYDRATE: 16G

CHOLESTEROL: 0MG

SODIUM: 85MG

You don't need to be in the wild, wild West to enjoy these beans. This is my more healthful version of the classic campfire beans. There's no lard in these, but the Fakin Bacon Bits and the barbecue sauce give these beans an authentic Western-style flavor.

MAKES 8 SERVINGS	PREPARATION TIME: 30 MINUTES

1 tablespoon olive oil

1 cup chopped onions

2 cups cooked or canned white beans

2 tablespoons Lightlife Fakin Bacon Bits

1 cup Josie's Barbecue Sauce (page 167), or your favorite prepared barbecue sauce

Sea salt and freshly ground black pepper

1. Preheat the oven to 350°F. In a heavy-duty, oven-safe skillet over medium heat, heat the olive oil. Add the onions and cook, stirring, until translucent, 3 to 4 minutes. Add the beans and bacon bits, and stir for 2 to 3 minutes. Add the barbecue sauce and stir. Season with salt and pepper. Reduce the heat to medium-low, and cook, stirring, for 2 to 3 minutes.

2. Place the beans in the oven for 15 to 20 minutes to bake in the flavors.

Totally dairy-free cooking

✳ OVEN-BAKED SPICED YUCA FRIES

After making these, you'll prove to your family and friends that you don't need a deep-fryer to make delicious crispy fries. Yukon Gold potatoes can be substituted for yuca if it's not available. Scrub the skin but do not peel these potatoes. Make extra fries because these are so good everyone will want seconds. Try them with Basic Ketchup (page 165).

CALORIES: 19.9

FAT: 2.3G

PROTEIN: 0G

CARBOHYDRATE: 0G

CHOLESTEROL: 0MG

SODIUM: 0MG

MAKES 6 SERVINGS　　　　PREPARATION TIME: 30 MINUTES

1 pound yuca, peeled, or large
　　unpeeled Yukon Gold potatoes
1 tablespoon olive oil
¼ teaspoon ground coriander

¼ teaspoon chili powder
Sea salt and freshly ground black
　　pepper

1. Preheat the oven to 400°F. In a mixing bowl, slice the yuca into 4-inch-long by ¼- to ½-inch-thick fries. Toss and coat thoroughly with the olive oil, coriander, chili powder, and salt and pepper to taste.

2. Place the yuca fries on nonstick baking tray and bake for 10 minutes. Turn over and bake for 10 minutes more. Serve immediately.

On the
Side

✳ ROASTED TARO ROOT

CALORIES: 153.1

FAT: 3.9G

PROTEIN: 1.7G

CARBOHYDRATE: 30G

CHOLESTEROL: 0MG

SODIUM: 12MG

Taro root is similar to a potato but with more exotic tones. It will spice up any of your fish or poultry dishes. It is especially nice with the Chilean Sea Bass with Chipotle Orange Glaze (page 97).

MAKES 4 SERVINGS	PREPARATION TIME: 35 MINUTES

1 pound piece of taro root, peeled, or large unpeeled Yukon Gold potato

Olive oil

Sea salt and freshly ground black pepper

Ground coriander

Preheat the oven to 350°F. Slice the taro into 4 to 5 thick slices and rub with the olive oil to taste. Add salt, pepper and coriander to taste. Bake for 25 to 30 minutes, or until soft in the center.

Totally dairy-free cooking

✳ SPICED SWEET POTATO AND CRANBERRY COUSCOUS

Couscous is a terrific and exotic grain. It's easy to make and very healthful. This version is a great side dish with a warm turkey dinner. You can also eat it cold the following day with whatever you are having for lunch. Use it as filler in your favorite wrap.

CALORIES: 278.6

FAT: 2.2G

PROTEIN: 7.6G

CARBOHYDRATE: 56.4G

CHOLESTEROL: 0MG

SODIUM: 9MG

MAKES 8 SERVINGS   **PREPARATION TIME: 30 MINUTES**

1 medium sweet potato, peeled and
   diced

½ teaspoon ground nutmeg

½ teaspoon ground cinnamon

1 tablespoon honey

2 teaspoons cider vinegar

1 pound couscous

2 ounces sun-dried cranberries

1 tablespoon canola oil

3 tablespoons maple syrup

Salt and freshly ground black pepper

10 fresh mint leaves, julienned

1. Fill a medium saucepan with 3¼ cups water. Bring to a boil and add the sweet potato. Reduce the heat and simmer for approximately 10 minutes, or until tender. Add the nutmeg, cinnamon, honey and vinegar to the water, and stir. Remove from the heat.

2. In a medium mixing bowl, place the couscous, cranberries, oil and maple syrup, and mix well. Pour the hot liquid with the potatoes over the couscous and mix thoroughly with a fork. Cover with plastic wrap and keep sealed for 5 minutes. Remove the plastic wrap and fluff with a fork. Season with salt, pepper and mint leaves.

On the
Side

Whether you're two or a hundred and two, some of your all-time favorite meals are probably loaded with fat, calories and lots of dairy. These revamped dairy-free versions are guaranteed to bring out the kid in everyone. Getting your kids off dairy early in life is important and helps them learn to eat a healthful diet and acquire good habits at a young age. At least 50 percent of all children in America are allergic to milk. Since kids have a propensity for colds, and since cow's milk is mucus forming, it adds to their stuffiness and congestion, so you may not even realize your child is allergic. Twenty percent of all babies suffer terribly because they are allergic to cow's milk. Simply switching their formula to a non-dairy version can help (many companies now offer calcium-enriched soy formulas). If you're feeding your kids a well-balanced diet, they will easily get all of the vitamins and nutrients they need without downing a big glass of milk at each meal.

✳ GRILLED SOY CHEDDAR CHEESE AND FAKIN BACON SANDWICH

CALORIES: 351.5

FAT: 14.3G

PROTEIN: 24.2G

CARBOHYDRATE: 32.8G

CHOLESTEROL: 1MG

SODIUM: 1087MG

I made this for Rosie O'Donnell on her show and she loved it. It's totally delicious and satisfies that comfort food craving we all get from time to time.

MAKES 2 SERVINGS   **PREPARATION TIME: 15 MINUTES**

4 ounces (6 slices) Lightlife Fakin
    Bacon
4 ounces soy cheddar cheese, sliced

4 slices spelt or 7-grain bread
1 teaspoon soy margarine

1. Preheat the toaster oven or regular oven to 350°F. Place the bacon and cheddar on top of 1 piece of bread. Cover with a second piece of bread.

2. Heat a medium nonstick skillet with ½ teaspoon of the margarine over medium heat. Place the sandwich in the pan when the margarine melts. Brown both sides of the sandwich and place in the oven to finish for 5 minutes. Repeat the process for the second sandwich.

NOTE: Put a heavy object like a can of tomatoes on top of the bread while grilling the sandwich for an old-fashioned griddle taste.

Totally
dairy-free
cooking

✳ OLD-FASHIONED BAKED MACARONI AND CHEESE

Old fashioned, but incredibly modern. Your kids will never know that you took out the dairy. Be sure to try out different soy cheeses to see which one your family likes best, but I like the Soya Kaas and Lisanatti Soy-Sation brands.

CALORIES: 196.6

FAT: 5.6G

PROTEIN: 11.8G

CARBOHYDRATE: 25.2G

CHOLESTEROL: 0MG

SODIUM: 321MG

MAKES 6 SERVINGS   **PREPARATION TIME: 40 MINUTES**

1 teaspoon soy margarine

1 clove garlic, minced

1 medium shallot, minced

½ cup chopped onions

1¼ cups plain soy milk

1 teaspoon arrowroot

½ cup grated soy cheddar

3 cups cooked macaroni elbows

2½ tablespoons soy Parmesan

Sea salt and freshly ground black
   pepper

1 tablespoon whole wheat bread
   crumbs

1. Preheat the oven to 350°F. Heat the margarine in a medium nonstick skillet over medium heat. Add the garlic and shallot and cook, stirring, until golden, about 1 minute. Add the onions and cook, stirring, until translucent, about 3 minutes. Add the soy milk and bring to a simmer.

2. Mix the arrowroot with 2 teaspoons of water and whisk into the soy milk mixture for 1 minute. Add the soy cheddar, whisking continuously. Toss in the pasta, 2 tablespoons of the soy Parmesan, and season with salt and pepper.

3. Transfer the mixture to a nonstick loaf pan. Sprinkle with the remaining ½ tablespoon Parmesan and the bread crumbs. Bake in the oven for 15 minutes. Serve warm. Cut in slices just like a meat loaf.

For Kids
of all
Ages

✳ 199

✳ PEANUT BUTTER, BANANA AND JELLY QUESADILLA

CALORIES: 158.9

FAT: 5.9G

PROTEIN: 3.9G

CARBOHYDRATE: 24.5G

CHOLESTEROL: 0MG

SODIUM: 132MG

This is a favorite late-night snack, especially when I just want some-thing sweet. It's crunchy, creamy and delicious. For pure decadence, try it with a little soy ice cream on top. Mmmm, now that's good!

MAKES 4 SERVINGS   **PREPARATION TIME: 12 MINUTES**

2 tablespoons peanut butter (no sugar, salt or oil added)

2 tablespoons fruit-sweetened preserves, any flavor

1 medium banana, sliced thin diagonally

Two 8-inch 7-grain tortillas

½ teaspoon soy margarine

1. On 1 tortilla, spread the peanut butter evenly, and top with the fruit preserves and sliced bananas. Place the second tortilla on top.

2. Heat a nonstick skillet over medium-low heat and melt the margarine. Place the quesadilla in the pan and brown both sides over medium-low heat. Adjust the flame to avoid burning one side before heating the ingredients in the center.

3. Place on a cutting board and slice into 8 pieces. Serve warm.

✳ SOY CINNAMON SPELT FRENCH TOAST

Kids have allergies to wheat almost as much as they do to dairy, so this is a nice break from traditional wheat bread. The cereal crumbs really set this apart from normal French toast and your kids will love the extra crunch. Serve with maple syrup, fruit "butter," cinnamon, bananas and strawberries. For a real treat, dab some Soy Whipped Cream (page 227) on top.

CALORIES: 231

FAT: 5G

PROTEIN: 7.3G

CARBOHYDRATE: 39.9G

CHOLESTEROL: 1MG

SODIUM: 546MG

MAKES: 4 SERVINGS   **PREPARATION TIME: 30 MINUTES**

1 cup lowfat vanilla soy milk

1 large egg white

1 tablespoon maple syrup

1 teaspoon sucanat sugar

⅛ teaspoon ground cinnamon

⅛ teaspoon ground nutmeg

¼ teaspoon sea salt

½ cup Barbara's Organic Corn Flakes
  or any other natural corn cereal
  with no refined sugar added

8 slices spelt or 7-grain bread

2 teaspoons soy margarine

1. Preheat the oven to 350°F. In a medium mixing bowl, whisk together the soy milk, egg white, maple syrup, sugar, cinnamon, nutmeg and salt.

2. In a coffee grinder or small food processor, grind the corn flakes to a medium chop and set aside in a small mixing bowl.

3. Dip the bread slices in the soy mixture for 2 minutes and transfer to the bowl of crushed corn flakes. Place the coated slices on a foil-lined baking tray.

4. Heat a nonstick skillet over medium heat with ¼ teaspoon of the soy margarine. Brown both sides of the bread, then place on a clean nonstick baking tray. Bake to finish cooking for 7 minutes or until the middle of the French toast is no longer soft.

For Kids
of all
Ages

✳ THREE-GRAIN SUPER PANCAKES

PER PANCAKE

CALORIES 112.4

FAT 2G

PROTEIN 5.4G

CARBOHYDRATE 20.2G

CHOLESTEROL 0MG

SODIUM 272MG

Place thinly sliced bananas, sliced strawberries, blueberries, dairy-free chocolate chips or carob chips in the pancake as one side is browning to create an array of flavors. Even the hardest-to-please kid will become a happy camper. You can replace the blue cornmeal with regular cornmeal or corn flour. Refrigerate the unused mix overnight and whisk with a little extra soy milk to have some incredible "leftover" pancakes or a great midnight snack if you can't wait until the next morning.

MAKES FIVE 6-INCH PANCAKES   **PREPARATION TIME: 15 MINUTES**

½ cup Arrowhead Mills spelt flour

¼ cup Arrowhead Mills soy flour

¼ cup Arrowhead Mills blue cornmeal

½ teaspoon baking powder

½ teaspoon baking soda

2 tablespoons egg whites (from about 1 egg)

½ teaspoon vanilla extract

¾ cup lowfat, vanilla soy milk

¼ teaspoon sea salt

1 tablespoon maple syrup, plus additional for serving

1. In a mixing bowl, add all of the ingredients and whisk together.

2. Spray a nonstick skillet or nonstick griddle with canola oil spray and heat over medium heat. Add about 3 tablespoons of batter to the skillet to make each 6-inch pancake. Turn after 2 to 3 minutes, or when golden. Cook on the other side for 2 to 3 minutes more.

3. Keep the oven warm at 200°F and place finished pancakes in it to keep warm if you are making a large amount at one time. Serve with maple syrup.

When buying cereals for your kids, look at the ingredients. Even some of the so-called natural cereals are filled with refined sugars. Look for evaporated cane sugar in the ingredients if you want to get a sweetened cereal.

Totally
dairy-free
cooking

✳ BLUEBERRY CORN MUFFINS

No one you serve these muffins to will ever believe they're healthful. They're so moist and have such a great flavor. They're lowfat and wheat-free, too! What more could you ask for in a muffin? Nuthin'!

PER MUFFIN

CALORIES 154.4

FAT 1.5G

PROTEIN 2.6G

CARBOHYDRATE: 27.2G

CHOLESTEROL 2MG

SODIUM 235MG

MAKES 12 MUFFINS   **PREPARATION TIME: 45 MINUTES**

6 ounces blueberry soy yogurt

2 ounces silken tofu

2 tablespoons unsweetened
    applesauce

10 tablespoons sucanat sugar

2 tablespoons egg whites (from
    about 1 egg)

1 cup fresh or thawed blueberries

1 teaspoon baking powder

½ teaspoon baking soda

1 cup corn flour

1 cup cornmeal

½ teaspoon sea salt

1. Preheat the oven to 400°F. In a mixing bowl, combine the yogurt, tofu, applesauce, sucanat and egg whites. Fold in the blueberries.

2. In another bowl, sift together the baking powder, baking soda, corn flour, cornmeal, and salt. Add the dry ingredients to the wet and gently combine.

3. Spray a nonstick muffin pan with canola oil spray. Evenly distribute the batter into 12 muffin cups. Bake for 22 to 24 minutes. Keep in a sealed container at room temperature for up to 3 days.

For Kids
of all
Ages

✳ BANANA–CHOCOLATE CHIP SPELT MUFFINS

PER MUFFIN

CALORIES: 204.4

FAT: 3.5G

PROTEIN: 3.6G

CARBOHYDRATE: 42.1G

CHOLESTEROL: 0MG

SODIUM: 253MG

These muffins are every bit as decadent as their dairy-laden cousins.

MAKES 12 MUFFINS   **PREPARATION TIME: 45 MINUTES**

1 cup mashed ripe bananas

½ cup soft tofu

¾ cup evaporated cane sugar

½ teaspoon sea salt

1 tablespoon egg whites (from about 1 egg)

2 teaspoons baking powder

1 teaspoon baking soda

2 cups Arrowhead Mills spelt flour

½ cup dairy-free chocolate chips

1. Preheat the oven to 350°F. In a mixing bowl, combine the bananas, tofu, sugar, salt and egg whites. Mix thoroughly. Add the baking powder, baking soda and flour. Mix gently. Stir in the chocolate chips.

2. Spray a nonstick muffin tin with canola oil spray. Evenly distribute the mixture into 12 muffin cups. Bake for 24 to 28 minutes. Store for up to 3 days in an airtight container.

Totally dairy-free cooking

✳ FIVE-MINUTE TUNA

This is a quick lowfat meal packed with protein that will keep your motor running all day long. Always use albacore, dolphin-safe tuna packed in water. Add your favorite sprouted vegetables for extra vitamins. Serve with rice crackers, spelt toast or in a wrap sandwich.

CALORIES: 114.3

FAT: 3.2G

PROTEIN: 18.4G

CARBOHYDRATE: 2.6G

CHOLESTEROL: 21MG

SODIUM: 384MG

MAKES 2 SERVINGS   **PREPARATION TIME: 5 MINUTES**

One 6-ounce can tuna (packed in water)

2 teaspoons Dijon mustard

2 teaspoons balsamic vinegar

1 teaspoon extra-virgin olive oil

½ teaspoon tamari soy sauce

1 tablespoon minced red onions

Sea salt and freshly ground black pepper

1 plum tomato, seeded and diced

Drain the tuna and put in a small mixing bowl. Add all the ingredients except the tomato. Using a fork, toss gently until well mixed. Fold in the tomatoes, check the seasoning and serve.

For Kids
of aLL
Ages

✳ 205

✳ SCRAMBLED TOFU WITH VEGETABLES

This is perfect for anyone who doesn't like eggs. It has a lot of protein to keep you going throughout the day. Try making a steaming breakfast tortilla wrap filled with the scrambled tofu, Guacamole (page 161), Tofu Sour Cream (page 163), and soy cheddar cheese. Don't forget to use your choice of fresh homemade salsas from this book.

MAKES 6 SERVINGS	PREPARATION TIME: 15 MINUTES

1 pound firm tofu

1 teaspoon ground turmeric

1 teaspoon minced garlic

½ cup minced onions

3 teaspoons Bragg's Liquid Amino, or tamari soy sauce

½ cup minced tomatoes

2 tablespoons minced bell peppers

½ cup sliced button mushrooms

Sea salt and freshly ground black pepper

2 tablespoons trimmed and thinly sliced scallions

1. Freeze the tofu in the original package for a minimum of 12 hours. Defrost the unopened package in warm water or overnight in the refrigerator. Drain the liquid from the package and press the tofu firmly between your hands to rid it of excess liquid. The finished tofu will resemble the texture of a damp sponge.

2. Crumble the tofu in a mixing bowl and sprinkle with the turmeric and mix well.

3. Spray a nonstick skillet with canola oil spray and set over medium heat. Add the garlic and onions and cook, stirring, until the onions are translucent, about 3 minutes. Add ¼ cup of water and 2 teaspoons of the Liquid Amino, and stir. Add the tomatoes, bell peppers and mushrooms, and cook, stirring, for 3 minutes. Add the tofu, and stir for an additional 4 to 5 minutes. Drizzle in ¼ cup water and the remaining 1 teaspoon Liquid Amino and stir for an additional 3 minutes. Season with salt and pepper to taste and top with the scallions.

Totally
dairy-free
Cooking

The first thing a nutritionist will tell you if you're trying to lose weight and improve your health is to cut out dairy, wheat and refined white sugar from your diet. All of the recipes in this chapter follow that philosophy and, incredibly, still taste great. I use wheat-free flours when I bake—spelt, oat and soy flours are actually *more* flavorful than the standard white wheat flour.

The average American adult consumes around 136 pounds of sugar a year. Refined white sugar is a stimulant that causes artificial highs and lows in most people's moods. The more refined a sugar is, the more chemically processed it is. It's simply an unhealthful food choice, and frankly isn't totally necessary to satisfy a craving for something sweet.

I've eliminated refined white sugar and dairy in all of these desserts so that you can still have your cake and eat it, too.

I use all natural sweeteners instead. They're much better for you and easier for your body to digest.

✳ ALMOND BISCOTTI

PER COOKIE

CALORIES: 131.6

FAT: 2.8G

PROTEIN: 2.6G

CARBOHYDRATE: 20.4G

CHOLESTEROL: 0MG

SODIUM: 156MG

This is my Uncle Frank Lanza's mother's recipe that I ate throughout my childhood. It was a real challenge to make it any better, so I made a more healthful version that tastes just like the original.

MAKES 28 BISCOTTI   **PREPARATION TIME: 1½ HOURS**

2 cups flour, preferably whole grain pastry flour

1 cup sucanat sugar

1 teaspoon sea salt

1 teaspoon baking soda

¼ cup slivered almonds

¼ cup vegetable oil, or almond oil

2 tablespoons egg whites (from about 1 egg)

¼ cup unsweetened applesauce

1 tablespoon maple syrup

1. Preheat the oven to 325°F. In a mixing bowl, mix together the flour, sugar, salt, baking soda and almonds.

2. In another bowl, mix together the oil, egg whites, applesauce and maple syrup. Add the wet ingredients to the dry, mixing thoroughly by hand.

3. Spray a nonstick baking tray with canola oil spray. Form the dough into 2 loaves, 2 to 3 inches wide. Bake for 20 to 22 minutes. Turn off the oven, remove the cookies, set the tray on a wire rack and cool 45 minutes.

4. Reheat the oven to 325°F. Cut the loaves into ½-inch slices and place on their sides on a clean nonstick cookie sheet. Bake 8 minutes. Cool on wire racks and store in an airtight container for up to 2 weeks.

Totally
dairy-free
cooking

✳ CORN AND SUN-DRIED CRANBERRY BISCOTTI

Don't get confused and use cornmeal in this recipe instead of corn flour. Cornmeal is coarser and will give you a grittier texture.

PER COOKIE

CALORIES: 100.7

FAT: 2.5G

PROTEIN: 1G

CARBOHYDRATE: 18.9G

CHOLESTEROL: 0MG

SODIUM: 124MG

MAKES 26 BISCOTTI   **PREPARATION TIME: 1⅓ HOURS**

2¼ cups corn flour

1 cup plus 2 tablespoons evaporated
    cane sugar

1 teaspoon baking soda

1 teaspoon sea salt

¼ teaspoon ground turmeric

¼ cup sun-dried cranberries

¼ cup plain soy yogurt

¼ cup canola oil

3 tablespoons egg whites (from 1 to
    2 eggs)

1 tablespoon maple syrup

1. Preheat the oven to 325°F. In a mixing bowl, sift together the flour, sugar, baking soda, salt and turmeric. Set aside.

2. In another bowl, combine the cranberries, soy yogurt, oil, egg whites and maple syrup. Fold in the flour mixture with a plastic spatula.

3. Spray a nonstick baking tray with canola oil spray. Form the dough into 2 loaves, 2 to 3 inches wide. Bake for 20 to 22 minutes. Turn off the oven, remove the cookies, set the tray on a wire rack and cool 45 minutes.

4. Reheat the oven to 325°F. On a cutting board, slice the loaves into ½-inch slices (12 per loaf) and place on their sides on a clean nonstick baking tray. Bake 8 minutes. Cool and store in an airtight container for up to 2 weeks.

De/erTs

PER COOKIE
CALORIES: 139
FAT: 3.3G
PROTEIN: 2.5G
CARBOHYDRATE: 25.9G
CHOLESTEROL: 0MG
SODIUM: 127MG

The flavor of chocolate and bananas has always been one of my favorites. Try these with Vanilla-Soy Cappuccino (page 233).

MAKES 26 BISCOTTI	PREPARATION TIME: 1¼ HOURS

1 cup Arrowhead Mills whole wheat pastry flour

1 cup Arrowhead Mills brown rice flour

¼ cup unsweetened carob powder

1 teaspoon baking soda

1 teaspoon sea salt

1 cup plus 2 tablespoons evaporated cane sugar

3 tablespoons egg whites (from 1 to 2 eggs)

¼ cup mashed, ripe banana

¼ cup canola oil

1. Preheat the oven to 325°F. In a mixing bowl, sift together the pastry flour, rice flour, carob powder, baking soda, salt and sugar. Set aside.

2. In another mixing bowl, blend together the egg whites, banana and oil. Fold in the flour mixture with a plastic spatula.

3. Spray a nonstick baking tray with canola oil spray. Form the dough into 2 loaves, 2 to 3 inches wide. Bake for 18 to 20 minutes. Turn off the oven, remove the cookies, set the tray on a wire rack and cool 45 minutes.

4. Reheat the oven to 325°F. On a cutting board, cut the loaves into ½-inch slices (12 per loaf) and place slices on their sides on a clean nonstick baking tray. Bake 6 to 8 minutes. Cool and store in an airtight container for up to 2 weeks in an airtight container.

Totally dairy-free Cooking

✳ ORANGE SPICED SPELT BISCOTTI

These Asian-inspired biscotti are a great accompaniment to a nice cup of Green Chai Tea (page 234).

PER COOKIE
CALORIES: 113
FAT: 2.4G
PROTEIN: 1.5G
CARBOHYDRATE: 21.3G
CHOLESTEROL: 0MG
SODIUM: 134MG

MAKES 24 BISCOTTI   **PREPARATION TIME: 1¼ HOURS**

2¼ cups spelt flour

1 cup plus 2 tablespoons evaporated
    cane sugar

1 teaspoon baking soda

1 teaspoon sea salt

1½ teaspoons ground coriander

1½ teaspoons ground ginger

3 tablespoons egg whites (from 1 to
    2 eggs)

¼ cup canola oil

¼ cup unsweetened applesauce

1 whole orange, zested and juiced

1. Preheat the oven to 325°F. In a mixing bowl, sift together the flour, sugar, baking soda, salt, coriander, and ginger. Set aside

2. In another mixing bowl, blend together the egg whites, oil, applesauce, orange zest and juice. Fold in the flour mixture with a plastic spatula.

3. Spray a nonstick baking tray with canola oil spray. Form the dough into 2 loaves, 2 to 3 inches wide. Bake for 20 to 22 minutes. Turn off the oven, remove the cookies, set the tray on a wire rack and cool 45 minutes.

4. Reheat the oven to 325°F. On a cutting board, cut the loaves into ½-inch slices (12 per loaf) and place on their sides on a clean nonstick baking tray. Bake 8 minutes. Cool and store in an airtight container for up to 2 weeks.

> Give the gift of health—pick up some pretty containers around the holidays and make these healthful treats and give them as gifts at parties and get-togethers.

DesserTs

✱ CHOCOLATE CHIP SPELT COOKIES

PER COOKIE

CALORIES: 133.8

FAT: 2.5G

PROTEIN: 2.2G

CARBOHYDRATE: 22G

CHOLESTEROL: 0MG

SODIUM: 109MG

Being a former traditional chocolate chip cookie lover, it was a challenge to make a dairy-free, lower fat version with the same delicious flavor that satisfied my cravings. Caution: Keep out of reach of children (of all ages)—they're dangerously good.

MAKES 18 COOKIES   **PREPARATION TIME: 30 MINUTES**

2 tablespoons soy margarine

¾ cup sucanat sugar

2 tablespoons egg whites (from about 1 egg)

2 ounces soft tofu

½ teaspoon sea salt

2 tablespoons unsweetened applesauce

½ teaspoon vanilla extract

½ cup dairy-free chocolate chips

1 cup plus 2 tablespoons Arrowhead Mills spelt flour

½ teaspoon baking powder

1. Preheat the oven to 375°F. In a mixing bowl, cream together the soy margarine and sucanat. Add the egg whites, tofu, salt, applesauce and vanilla and mix thoroughly. Fold in the chocolate chips.

2. In another bowl, sift the flour and baking powder together. Mix into the wet ingredients with a plastic spatula.

3. Spray a nonstick cookie sheet with canola oil spray. Place teaspoon-size dollops of the dough on the cookie sheet. Bake for 12 to 15 minutes. Store up to 10 days in an airtight container.

Totally dairy-free Cooking

✳ PEANUT BUTTER, MILLET AND OAT FLOUR COOKIES

The ultimate test of this recipe was getting my father's approval because he's a peanut butter fanatic. But, after a lot of tries, Dad signed off on this one. It's important to use natural peanut butter for this recipe. You can try either creamy or chunky peanut butter for different textures, depending on your taste, but make sure there's no added sugar, salt or oil in the brand you buy.

PER COOKIE:

CALORIES: 154.5

FAT: 4.5G

PROTEIN: 3.5G

CARBOHYDRATE: 24.7G

CHOLESTEROL: 0MG

SODIUM: 149MG

MAKES 20 COOKIES　　　　　　　　**PREPARATION TIME: 30 MINUTES**

4 tablespoons soy margarine

½ cup sucanat sugar

½ cup evaporated cane sugar

2 ounces soft tofu

3 tablespoons peanut butter (no sugar, salt or oil added)

2 tablespoons egg whites (from about 1 egg)

½ teaspoon vanilla extract

½ teaspoon sea salt

¾ cup Arrowhead Mills millet flour

¾ cup Arrowhead Mills oat flour

½ teaspoon baking soda

1. Preheat the oven to 375°F. In a mixing bowl, combine the margarine, sucanat and cane sugar. Mix in the tofu, peanut butter, egg whites, vanilla and salt.

2. In another bowl, sift together the millet and oat flours with the baking soda. Mix the dry ingredients into the wet mixture.

3. Spray a nonstick cookie sheet with canola oil spray. Place teaspoon-size dollops of dough on the cookie sheet. Bake for 12 to 14 minutes. Store in an airtight container for up to 10 days.

DESERTS

✳ 215

✳ OATMEAL COOKIES

PER COOKIE

CALORIES: 157.6

FAT: 2.8G

PROTEIN: 3.8G

CARBOHYDRATE: 26.6G

CHOLESTEROL: 0MG

SODIUM: 115MG

Put a couple of extra cookies in your kid's lunch so he or she can share their good fortune with their friends.

MAKES 36 COOKIES   **PREPARATION TIME: 40 MINUTES**

1½ cups sucanat sugar

4 tablespoons soy margarine

3 ounces soft tofu

5 tablespoons unsweetened
   applesauce

2 tablespoons egg whites (from
   about 1 egg)

1 teaspoon vanilla extract

Grated zest of 1 orange

2½ cups oat flour

½ teaspoon baking powder

½ teaspoon baking soda

½ teaspoon sea salt

2 cups quick-cooking rolled oats

½ cup raisins

1. Preheat the oven to 375°F. In a mixing bowl, mix together the sucanat, soy margarine, tofu and applesauce thoroughly. Add the egg whites, vanilla and orange zest, and mix.

2. In another mixing bowl, sift together the flour, baking powder, baking soda and salt. Add the oats and mix thoroughly.

3. Add the dry ingredients to the wet mixture, and lightly blend with a plastic spatula. Add the raisins, and stir with the spatula to mix.

4. Spray a nonstick cookie sheet with canola oil spray. Put teaspoon-size dollops of the dough on the cookie sheet. Bake for 18 to 20 minutes, until golden brown. Store up to 10 days in an airtight container.

Totally
dairy-free
cooking

✳ PEANUT BUTTER AND JELLY COOKIES

These are as fun to make as they are to eat. If you like peanut butter and jelly sandwiches, these are for you.

PER COOKIE

CALORIES: 123.4

FAT: 4G

PROTEIN: 3.6G

CARBOHYDRATE: 21.6G

CHOLESTEROL: 0MG

SODIUM: 175MG

MAKES 20 COOKIES   **PREPARATION TIME: 40 MINUTES**

2 cups Arrowhead Mills spelt flour

1 teaspoon baking soda

1 teaspoon sea salt

¼ cup creamy or crunchy peanut
  butter (no sugar, salt or oil added)

5 tablespoons maple syrup

1 tablespoon egg whites

3 tablespoons unsweetened
  applesauce

3 tablespoons canola oil

2 tablespoons lowfat, vanilla soy milk

5 teaspoons fruit-sweetened
  preserves, any flavor

1. Preheat the oven to 375°F. In a mixing bowl, sift together the flour and baking soda.

2. In another mixing bowl, combine the salt, peanut butter, maple syrup, egg whites, applesauce, canola oil and soy milk. Mix in the flour mixture with a plastic spatula.

3. Spray a nonstick baking tray with canola oil spray. Form the dough into 20 balls and place each one on the tray. Using your thumb, make a indentation in the center of the dough ball. Spoon in ¼ teaspoon of preserves and bake for 10 to 12 minutes. Store up to 2 weeks in an airtight container.

Desserts

✳ BANANA BREAD PUDDING

CALORIES: 492.7

FAT: 5.7G

PROTEIN: 9.1G

CARBOHYDRATE: 94.8G

CHOLESTEROL: 0MG

SODIUM: 490MG

This is a lowfat version of America's favorite comfort dessert, guaranteed to make any dairy-free skeptic a believer. Serve with Healthier Chocolate Sauce (page 226), Soy Caramel Sauce (page 225) or fresh strawberries with Soy Whipped Cream (page 227) for an added taste.

MAKES 8 SERVINGS **PREPARATION TIME: 1 HOUR AND 10 MINUTES**

1 liter lowfat, vanilla soy milk (about 4 cups)

1 cup sucanat sugar

2 tablespoons egg whites (from about 1 egg)

4 ripe bananas, pureed or mashed

1 cup raisins

One 1½-pound loaf spelt bread, or whole wheat bread

2 teaspoons ground cinnamon

1. Preheat the oven to 325°F. In a saucepan, heat the soy milk over medium heat, but do not boil. Add the sucanat and egg whites, and stir. Add the bananas and raisins, and stir. Remove from the heat.

2. Cube the bread and place in a mixing bowl. Pour the soy milk mixture over the bread. Place the mixture in a nonstick loaf pan. Sprinkle with the cinnamon.

3. Bake for 50 minutes. Serve warm. Store in your refrigerator for up to 3 days in an airtight container.

Totally dairy-free cooking

✳ VANILLA SOY TAPIOCA PUDDING

This dairy-free version is just as rich and tasty as the original without all the added calories and fat. Serve with fresh fruit or make a layered parfait with your favorite Jell-O.

CALORIES: 101.6

FAT: 1.2G

PROTEIN: 1.7G

CARBOHYDRATE: 22G

CHOLESTEROL: 0MG

SODIUM: 128MG

MAKES 8 SERVINGS	PREPARATION TIME: 30 MINUTES, PLUS 2 HOURS SOAKING AND 4 HOURS REFRIGERATION

1 cup uncooked tapioca

2 cups lowfat vanilla soy milk

1 teaspoon vanilla extract

2 tablespoons maple syrup

½ teaspoon sea salt

2 teaspoons arrowroot

1. In a bowl, soak the tapioca in 1½ cups of water for 2 hours.

2. In a medium saucepan over medium heat, bring 1½ cups of water and the soy milk to a simmer. Add the tapioca, vanilla, maple syrup and salt. Simmer gently for 10 minutes, stirring frequently to avoid burning.

3. Meanwhile, in a small mixing bowl, mix together the arrowroot with 1 tablespoon water and add it to the simmering pudding. Simmer for 3 to 5 minutes more, stirring frequently.

4. Refrigerate the pudding for at least 4 hours before serving. Store in your refrigerator for up to 4 days in an airtight container.

DESSERTS

✳ JASMINE RICE AND BANANA PUDDING

CALORIES: 314.7

FAT: 2.2G

PROTEIN: 6.1G

CARBOHYDRATE: 60.5G

CHOLESTEROL: 0MG

SODIUM: 91MG

You can substitute risotto rice, brown rice or even good old white rice in this recipe. The jasmine rice has a sweeter, more exotic flavor and is available in Asian markets. Remember to adjust the cooking time according to the rice you are using. Pour 1 to 2 ounces of vanilla soy milk over the pudding to bring back the creaminess when serving it chilled. Sprinkle a little cinnamon on top or try mixing it with your favorite sun-dried fruit.

MAKES 8 SERVINGS	PREPARATION TIME: 45 MINUTES

2 cups jasmine rice

3 cups vanilla soy milk

2 ripe bananas, pureed

1 teaspoon ground cinnamon

½ cup sucanat sugar

2 teaspoons arrowroot

2 tablespoons maple syrup

1. In a medium, heavy-bottomed saucepan, mix 4 cups of water with the rice. Bring to a boil, then reduce the heat and simmer for 5 minutes.

2. In a separate small saucepan over medium heat, heat the soy milk, bananas, sugar and cinnamon, but do not boil. Add this mixture to the rice. Simmer, stirring frequently to avoid burning the bottom, for about 15 minutes, until the rice is soft.

3. In a small bowl, mix together the arrowroot and 1 tablespoon water and add to the cooked rice pudding. Cook, stirring, for 5 to 7 minutes.

4. Place the mixture in a storage container and let it cool slightly. Serve warm, drizzled with the maple syrup. Store in the refrigerator for up to 3 days in an airtight container.

Totally dairy-free cooking

✳ HEALTHIER PIE CRUST

You can make extra crusts and freeze them. Roll them up and place them in a freezer bag to keep them fresh. Defrost them in the refrigerator for 4 to 6 hours in the freezer bag.

PER ⅛ OF PIE

CALORIES: 128.1

FAT: 3.6G

PROTEIN: 3.8G

CARBOHYDRATE: 21.1G

CHOLESTEROL: 0MG

SODIUM: 72MG

MAKES ONE 9-INCH PIE CRUST   PREPARATION TIME: 30 MINUTES

½ cup whole wheat pastry flour

¼ cup oat flour

½ cup spelt flour

⅛ teaspoon sea salt

1 tablespoon sucanat sugar

1 tablespoon soft tofu

1 tablespoon soy margarine

Mix together the flours, salt and sugar in a food processor and pulse for 1 minute. Add the tofu and margarine and mix for 2 minutes. Add 6 tablespoons cold water and mix for 1 minute more. Remove from the processor and form into a ball. Roll out approximately a 10-inch circle and press into a 9-inch pie pan. It can be used immediately or frozen at this point if you place it in a freezer bag.

DeSSerTs

✳ MACADAMIA APPLE PIE

I tried to take this off the menu at Josie's when apples were out of season, but the demand was so high, I had to keep it on year-round. This is truly an all-American favorite, and it's great with vanilla soy ice cream on top drizzled with a little Soy Caramel Sauce (page 225) for a dairy-free à la mode.

MAKES 8 SERVINGS   **PREPARATION TIME: 1½ HOURS**

Always defrost frozen desserts while they are still wrapped in the freezer bag. This way the moisture will condense on the outside of the bag and not on the food.

1 recipe Healthier Pie Crust (page 221)

7 Granny Smith apples, peeled

6 tablespoons sucanat sugar

2 teaspoons ground cinnamon

⅛ teaspoon sea salt

½ cup plus 1 tablespoon whole wheat flour

½ cup quick-cooking rolled oats

¼ cup macadamia nuts

2 tablespoons unsweetened applesauce

2 tablespoons soy margarine

1. Preheat the oven to 300°F. Roll out the pie dough and place in a 9-inch pie dish. Set aside.

2. Thinly slice the peeled apples and toss them in a bowl with 2 tablespoons of the sucanat, the cinnamon, salt and 1 tablespoon of the flour.

3. In another mixing bowl, mix together the remaining ½ cup flour and the oats. Mix in the remaining 4 tablespoons sucanat, the macadamia nuts, applesauce and soy margarine.

4. Put the apples into the uncooked pie shell and layer the oat topping over the filling. Bake for 1 hour. Serve warm. Store in your refrigerator for up to 3 days in an airtight container.

Totally
dairy-free
cooking

✳ PEAR STRAWBERRY PIE

Using this basic recipe, experiment with different seasonal fruits from rhubarb to papaya, berries and even bananas. It's delicious served with vanilla soy ice cream.

CALORIES: 329.4

FAT: 11.4G

PROTEIN: 5.1G

CARBOHYDRATE: 51G

CHOLESTEROL: 12MG

SODIUM: 131MG

MAKES 8 SERVINGS　　　　　　　　**PREPARATION TIME: 1½ HOURS**

4 cups peeled and chopped pears

2 tablespoons fruit juice concentrate,
　or maple syrup

2 tablespoons arrowroot

1 pint strawberries, stemmed and
　halved

1 recipe Healthier Pie Crust
　(page 221)

½ cup whole wheat flour

½ cup quick-cooking rolled oats

¼ cup sucanat sugar

⅛ teaspoon sea salt

4 tablespoons chopped walnuts

2 tablespoons unsweetened
　applesauce

2 tablespoons soy margarine

1. Preheat the oven to 300°F. In a nonstick skillet over medium heat, cook the pears for 2 to 3 minutes, then add the fruit juice. Continue cooking for 10 to 12 minutes until the exterior of the fruit is soft. Mix the arrowroot with 2 tablespoons of water, add to the pears and cook for an additional 2 to 3 minutes. Transfer the pears to a mixing bowl and fold in the strawberries.

2. Roll out the pie dough and place in a 9-inch pie pan. Set aside.

3. In a mixing bowl, mix together the flour, rolled oats, sucanat, salt, chopped walnuts, applesauce and margarine.

4. Place the fruit filling in the uncooked pie crust and layer the flour-oat topping over the filling. Bake for 50 minutes. Serve warm. Store in your refrigerator for up to 3 days in an airtight container.

DeSerTs

✳ 223

✳ SPICED PUMPKIN–TOFU PIE

CALORIES: 250.2

FAT: 7.3G

PROTEIN: 4.9G

CARBOHYDRATE: 32.6G

CHOLESTEROL: 0MG

SODIUM: 286MG

Don't forget about this on Thanksgiving. If you eat too much and can't fit this in with the meal, it makes a great lowfat midnight snack. Canned pumpkin is used in this recipe so you can serve it year-round. Tofu makes it extra creamy.

MAKES 8 SERVINGS   **PREPARATION TIME: 1 HOUR, PLUS 2 HOURS FOR COOLING**

1 teaspoon ground cinnamon

½ teaspoon ground ginger

½ teaspoon ground nutmeg

⅔ cup sucanat sugar

⅛ teaspoon sea salt

3 tablespoons egg whites (from 1 to 2 eggs)

2 cups canned pumpkin puree (approximately one 15-ounce can) (see Note)

8 ounces soft tofu (1 cup)

2 tablespoons arrowroot

1 recipe Healthier Pie Crust (page 221)

1. Preheat the oven to 350°F. In a mixing bowl, whisk together the spices, sucanat and salt. Mix in the egg whites, pumpkin, tofu and arrowroot. An electric mixer can be used if you have one, otherwise use a whisk and elbow grease.

2. Place the pie crust in a 9-inch pie dish. Pour the filling into the pie crust. Bake for 50 to 60 minutes, or until set. Cool for at least 2 hours before serving. Store in your refrigerator for up to 4 days in an airtight container.

NOTE: To use fresh pumpkin, cut it into pieces and roast in a 350°F oven for 40 to 50 minutes or boil the pieces in water for 20 to 30 minutes. Then peel off the tough outer skin and puree it in a food processor.

Totally
dairy-free
Cooking

✳ SOY CARAMEL SAUCE

I served this to Rosie O'Donnell in front of millions of people, and it fooled her. She couldn't get over the fact that she was eating a totally dairy-free sundae! To make a Soy Banana Split, slice bananas into a serving dish and add to 2 scoops of your favorite soy ice cream. Drizzle the caramel sauce over the top.

PER ¼ CUP
CALORIES: 218.4
FAT: 3.4G
PROTEIN: 0.9G
CARBOHYDRATE: 31.2G
CHOLESTEROL: 0MG
SODIUM: 200MG

MAKES 2 CUPS   **PREPARATION TIME: 20 MINUTES**

1 cup sucanat sugar

1 cup lowfat vanilla soy milk

½ cup brown rice syrup (see Note)

1 teaspoon vanilla extract

1 pinch sea salt

1 tablespoon arrowroot

2 tablespoons soy margarine

1. In a small, heavy-duty saucepan, combine the sucanat, soy milk, rice syrup, vanilla and salt. Bring to a boil, then reduce the heat and simmer for 3 minutes, whisking to prevent burning.

2. In a small bowl, mix together the arrowroot with 1 tablespoon of water and add to the sauce. Simmer for an additional 2 to 3 minutes. Remove from the flame and whisk in the margarine. Store in your refrigerator for up to 2 weeks in an airtight container.

NOTE: If you want to substitute the brown rice syrup with maple syrup, add an extra ½ tablespoon of arrowroot.

Desserts

✳ 225

✳ HEALTHIER CHOCOLATE SAUCE

This is a terrific dairy-free chocolate sauce. It has a multitude of uses. Serve warm as a dipping sauce for fresh fruit and berries, using fondue skewers. Or serve warm as a dipping sauce for one of the biscotti recipes in this book. It's also a great topping for a soy ice cream sundae.

MAKES 8 2-OUNCE SERVINGS   **PREPARATION TIME: 20 MINUTES**

1 cup sucanat sugar   ½ cup unsweetened cocoa

1 cup lowfat vanilla soy milk   1 tablespoon arrowroot

1. In a small, heavy-duty saucepan, combine the sucanat, soy milk and cocoa and bring to a boil. Reduce the heat and simmer for 4 to 5 minutes, stirring with a wire whip to avoid burning. Mix the arrowroot with 1 tablespoon of water, add to the cocoa mixture and continue to cook for 2 to 3 minutes.

2. Serve heated or at room temperature. Store in the refrigerator for up to 2 weeks in an airtight container.

✳ SOY WHIPPED CREAM

Maple syrup is a must for this recipe. It is the key to the flavor. This can be used on anything that you would ordinarily put whipped cream on.

PER ¼ CUP

CALORIES: 59.7

FAT: 2G

PROTEIN: 3.3G

CARBOHYDRATE: 8.1G

CHOLESTEROL: 0MG

SODIUM: 123MG

MAKES 2 CUPS	PREPARATION TIME: 20 MINUTES, PLUS 1 HOUR REFRIGERATION

10 ounces firm tofu

½ cup lowfat vanilla soy milk

½ teaspoon sea salt

6 tablespoons maple syrup

Cut the tofu in small pieces and place in a food processor. Add the soy milk, salt and maple syrup. Process until smooth. Refrigerate for 1 hour before serving. Store in the refrigerator for up to 3 days in an airtight container.

Desserts

The recipes in this chapter are guaranteed to wipe off your milk mustache . . . for good! Since you're getting healthier with your food choices, remember that you can get healthier with your drink selections, too. When I'm on the run, I'll drink a fruit smoothie or espresso with added protein powder and I get all the nutrients of a meal. Be careful when buying a protein powder because many of them contain whey, which is a dairy derivative. You want to buy a powder that is labeled "dairy free." Vegetable protein powders are very healthful and packed with essential vitamins and minerals. They are also very low in carbohydrates. Naturade is a high-protein, low-carbohydrate, dairy-free vegetable protein powder that will give you the necessary energy to start your day. It's an optional ingredient in any of the smoothies, but the added protein is a great way to stay strong all day long. Soy protein powders come in a myriad of flavors. Spiru-Tein is a brand that I like and they offer vanilla, chocolate, mocha, strawberry and plain powders.

✳ BREAKFAST OF CHAMPIONS

CALORIES: 204.9
FAT: 0.6G
PROTEIN: 26.2G
CARBOHYDRATE: 27.7G
CHOLESTEROL: 0MG
SODIUM: 298MG

I drink this every morning the way I would a cup of coffee. I prefer to drink this on an empty stomach, and then I wait one hour before eating any solid food. It really gets my metabolism started and peaks my energy for a great way to start the day.

MAKES 1 SERVING   **PREPARATION TIME: 5 MINUTES**

1 tablespoon Ultra Green Defense (Probiotic Formula)

2 tablespoons Naturade Vegetable Protein Powder

1 package Alacer E-mergen-C plus minerals (6 grams)

1 banana, peeled and frozen

1 cup chilled water

Put all the ingredients in a blender and puree until smooth. Serve immediately.

✳ FROZEN SOY-BANANA CAPPUCCINO

CALORIES: 98
FAT: 1.4G
PROTEIN: 2.2G
CARBOHYDRATE: 21.1G
CHOLESTEROL: 0MG
SODIUM: 9MG

This is a fantastic twist on regular cappuccino. The banana gives this coffee drink a sweeter and thicker texture. As an option, serve with 1 to 2 tablespoons of Naturade Vegetable Protein Powder for a pre-workout meal that will keep you buzzing through your day.

MAKES 2 SERVINGS   **PREPARATION TIME: 10 MINUTES**

¼ cup brewed espresso coffee

1 banana, peeled and frozen

½ cup lowfat, vanilla soy milk

1 tablespoon maple syrup, optional

Ice

In a blender, puree all the ingredients with ice to taste, and serve.

Totally
dairy-free
cooking

✳ VANILLA-SOY CAPPUCCINO

The flavor of the vanilla gives this twist on traditional cappuccino a slight marshmallow taste. If you really have a sweet tooth, try adding a dash of maple syrup. On a hot humid summer day, try making iced soy cappuccino. Simply pour your cappuccino into a glass of ice and you're ready to go.

CALORIES: 39.6

FAT: 2.3G

PROTEIN: 3.3G

CARBOHYDRATE: 2.2G

CHOLESTEROL: 0MG

SODIUM: 14MG

MAKES 1 SERVING   **PREPARATION TIME: 10 MINUTES**

2 shots (approximately 6 tablespoons) brewed espresso

½ cup lowfat, vanilla soy milk

Put the espresso in a coffee mug. Heat the soy milk to 140°F to 150°F, but do not boil. Pour over the espresso, and serve. Lowfat soy milk steams better than regular soy milk.

Drinks

CALORIES: 73

FAT: 1G

PROTEIN: 1.1G

CARBOHYDRATE: 12.8G

CHOLESTEROL: 0MG

SODIUM: 69MG

Serve this chai tea hot with the Orange Spiced Spelt Biscotti (page 213).

MAKES 2¼ CUPS CONCENTRATED TEA, OR 6 SERVINGS   PREPARATION TIME: 12 MINUTES

4 thin slices fresh ginger
⅛ teaspoon ground cardamom
¼ teaspoon ground anise seed
¼ teaspoon ground cinnamon
2 tablespoons sucanat sugar
3 tablespoons fruit juice concentrate,
    or honey

6 green tea bags (Celestial
    Seasonings is good)
2¼ cups lowfat almond milk or vanilla
    soy milk

1. Heat 2½ cups of water in a small saucepan with the ginger, cardamom, anise and cinnamon. Bring to a boil, then reduce the heat and simmer for 2 to 3 minutes. Add the sucanat and fruit juice concentrate. Simmer for 2 to 3 minutes more and remove from the stove. Steep the tea bags in the spice mixture for 5 minutes. Strain into a container and store for up to 1 week.

2. To serve, mix the tea concentrate with the almond milk and heat in a small saucepan, but do not boil. To prepare a single cup, mix equal parts of the tea concentrate with almond milk.

Totally
dairy-free
cooking

✳ BLACK CHAI TEA

This tea is absolutely incredible. It's rich, satisfying and has just enough caffeine in it to give you a jump start if needed. Try steaming the soy milk and making a chai soy cappuccino. Look out, Starbucks! Serve the hot tea with Carob Banana Biscotti (page 212).

CALORIES: 95.9

FAT: 1.8G

PROTEIN: 2.8G

CARBOHYDRATE: 14.6G

CHOLESTEROL: 0MG

SODIUM: 54MG

MAKES 2¼ CUPS CONCENTRATED TEA OR 6 SERVINGS   PREPARATION TIME: 12 MINUTES

½ teaspoon vanilla extract
½ teaspoon ground cinnamon
½ teaspoon ground cloves
⅛ teaspoon ground cardamom
3 tablespoons sucanat sugar
2 tablespoons honey

6 black tea bags (Celestial Seasonings Vanilla Maple Black Tea is good)
2¼ cups lowfat almond milk, or vanilla soy milk

1. Heat 2¼ cups of water in a small saucepan and add the vanilla, cinnamon, cloves and cardamom. Bring to a boil, reduce the heat, and simmer for 2 to 3 minutes. Add the sucanat and honey. Simmer for 2 to 3 minutes more, and remove from the stove. Steep the tea bags in the mixture for 5 minutes. Strain into a container and store for up to 7 days.

2. To serve hot, mix the tea concentrate with the almond milk and heat in a small saucepan, but do not boil. To prepare a single serving, mix equal parts of the tea concentrate with low-fat almond milk or vanilla soy milk and heat in a small pan, but do not boil.

To serve cold, chill the concentrate and serve with equal amounts of low-fat almond or vanilla soy milk over ice.

Experiment with different milk substitutes to find out which one works best for you. Soy, rice, almond and oat milks can be used interchangeably in any of these drinks. Unlike milk, soy milk does not have an expiration date on the box. Once opened, soy milk will last for ten days in the refrigerator.

Drinks

✳ 235

✳ HOT SPICED SOY APPLE CIDER

CALORIES: 129

FAT: 1.6G

PROTEIN: 2.2G

CARBOHYDRATE: 29.8G

CHOLESTEROL: 0MG

SODIUM: 14MG

This delicious apple cider will whisk your imagination to the Swiss Alps for an après-ski experience to remember. If you wear a fake cast and hang out around the fire, you're guaranteed to make friends.

MAKES 6 SERVINGS   **PREPARATION TIME: 30 MINUTES**

2 cups apple cider

One ½-inch piece fresh ginger, peeled and sliced

4 cinnamon sticks

½ cup fresh orange juice (from about 2 oranges)

6 tablespoons maple syrup

1½ cups lowfat almond, vanilla, or plain soy milk

1. In a saucepan over medium heat, heat the cider with the ginger and cinnamon sticks. Add the orange juice and maple syrup. Let mull for 15 minutes over low heat—do not bring to a boil.

2. Add the soy milk and serve in coffee mugs with cinnamon sticks.

Totally dairy-free Cooking

✳ STRAWBERRY BLUEBERRY SMOOTHIE

The very berry flavor of this smoothie is refreshing on a warm summer day or after a great workout. You can substitute any berry you like for a twist on this smoothie.

CALORIES: 126.5
FAT: 0.5G
PROTEIN: 1G
CARBOHYDRATE: 31.8G
CHOLESTEROL: 0MG
SODIUM: 4MG

MAKES 2 SERVINGS　　　　　　　　**PREPARATION TIME: 5 MINUTES**

½ cup fresh or frozen strawberries
½ cup fresh or frozen blueberries
½ cup apple juice
½ cup fresh orange juice (from about
　2 oranges)

2 tablespoons Naturade Vegetable
　Protein Powder, optional

Put all ingredients into a blender and puree until smooth.

NOTE: Freeze cleaned fruit like bananas, strawberries, mangoes and peaches, when they are ripe. This will eliminate the need for adding ice when making smoothies.

✳ BANANA–PEANUT BUTTER SMOOTHIE

Elvis would have loved this . . . so will your kids. It's better than any milk shake.

CALORIES: 145.1
FAT: 5.9G
PROTEIN: 4.9G
CARBOHYDRATE: 21G
CHOLESTEROL: 0MG
SODIUM: 58MG

MAKES 2 SERVINGS　　　　　　　　**PREPARATION TIME: 5 MINUTES**

1 banana
1 tablespoon peanut butter (no
　sugar, salt or oil added)
2 teaspoons maple syrup

6 ounces lowfat vanilla soy milk
8 ice cubes
2 tablespoons Naturade Vegetable
　Protein Powder, optional

Put all the ingredients into a blender with ¼ cup water and puree until smooth.

Drinks

INDEX

Index

240 *

INDex

kabocha squash soup, roasted, 47
ketchup, basic, 165

lemon caper soy "beurre blanc," seared
    halibut with, 91
lentil, roasted wild mushroom and walnut
    pâté, 24
lime miso basil pesto, 147
linguine with tuna Bolognese sauce, 76
lobster:
    butternut squash and asparagus stir-fry,
        100
    corn and jalapeño soy Jack quesadilla,
        36
    mango, avocado and asparagus spring
        roll, 35
    stock, 51
    sweet potato and corn bisque, 52

macadamia apple pie, 222
macaroni:
    and cheese, old-fashioned baked, 199
    corn, with soy jalapeño Jack and
        vegetables, baked, 106
mango:
    lobster, avocado and asparagus spring
        roll, 35
    —red miso dipping sauce, 150
    tomato and black bean salsa, 153
margarita chicken paillard, 129
marsala fettuccine, with breast of chicken,
    80
"meat" balls, millet and wild mushroom,
    116
meatballs, zesty turkey, 132
meat loaf:
    brown rice, red bean and vegetable, 111
    grain and vegetable, 112–113
    Southwestern turkey, 133
    spiced chicken, 134
meat substitutes, 14
mesclun greens:
    with balsamic mustard vinaigrette, 68
    with red wine–mustard vinaigrette, 65
milk substitutes, 18–19
millet:
    in grain and vegetable meat loaf,
        112–113
    peanut butter and oat flour cookies, 215
    and wild mushroom "meat" balls, 116
miso:
    -glazed eggplant, sweet, 186
    -pumpkin seed–basil pesto, 172

miso, barley:
    basil lime pesto, 147
    broth with tofu and vegetables, 46
    tofu vinaigrette, sesame seared tuna
        with, 96
miso, red:
    —mango dipping sauce, 150
    wasabi coulis, 149
monkfish "osso buco" with tomato saffron
    soy sauce, 90
muffins:
    banana-chocolate chip spelt, 204
    blueberry corn, 203
mushroom:
    au jus, rosemary, 146
    enoki, duck and celery soup, 44
    sauce, wild about, 143
    shiitake, chicken soup with parsnips
        and, 42
mushroom(s), portobello:
    fajitas, 111
    roasted, and soy mozzarella melt, 108
mushroom, wild:
    and millet "meat" balls, 116
    roasted, pâté of lentil, walnut and,
        24
    —roasted eggplant cakes, 28–29
    soup with tarragon, puree of, 55
mustard:
    balsamic vinaigrette, mesclun greens
        with, 68
    —red wine vinaigrette, mesclun greens
        with, 66

New England–style clam chowder,
    48–49

oat(meal):
    cookies, 216
    flour, peanut butter and millet cookies,
        215
    -spelt pizza dough, 82
oils, 14–15
onion:
    sweet potato and carrot dipping sauce,
        173
    tempeh bacon, soy cheddar and tomato
        quesadilla, 107
orange:
    chipotle glaze, Chilean sea bass with,
        97
    spiced spelt biscotti, 213
organic foods, 11–12

Index

* 243

INDEX

244 ✳

INDex